A Peewit in
WARTIME

A Peewit in
WARTIME

A Child's War in Somerset

Gordon Rendell

ryelands

First published in Great Britain in 2022

British Library Cataloguing-in-Publication Data
A CIP record for this title is available from the British Library

ISBN 978 1 90655 140 7

Halsgrove
Halsgrove House,
Ryelands Business Park,
Bagley Road, Wellington, Somerset TA21 9PZ
Tel: 01823 653777   Fax: 01823 216796
email: sales@halsgrove.com

Part of the Halsgrove group of companies
Information on all Halsgrove titles is available at: www.halsgrove.com

Printed and bound in India by Parksons Graphics Ltd

CONTENTS

To Phil and Angie Hodges, without whose skill and enthusiasm, this project would have been much more difficult to achieve. Phil, with his skilful ability to rescue and produce pictures out of rubbish photographs and Angie with her proof reading and pertinent criticism.

Thanks.

Why Peewit?

When my father was a boy, in the early nineteen hundreds, people from the local villages had nicknames. Hardington was inhabited in the spring and summer by hordes of green plovers, also called lapwings. or more commonly peewits, from the cry they made. As a result, people who came from Hardington were known as Peewits.

An adjoining village to the north-west, East Chinnock, was low-lying in a valley with a stream running through it called Chinnock Brook. This was the habitat of a certain plant which was the main food for a particular caterpillar loved by the young cuckoos, resulting in a more than usual number of these birds. The amazing thing about the young cuckoo is that unlike the juvenile swallow which heads off to Africa with its parents, the adult cuckoo has left for Africa weeks before these youngsters can fly, so how do they know which way to go? Anyway, people from East Chinnock were known as cuckoos.

Finally, West Coker lads to the north of Hardington were known as Hounds, Long Dogs, or Tall Boys, even my father couldn't explain why.

Since the war all these names seem to have disappeared. The application of artificial fertiliser to the fields at Hardington, I presume, is the reason for the disappearance of the peewits and the subsequent run-off into Chinnock Brook has seen the demise of the caterpillar's diet and therefore the cuckoos.

With little opposition, the Coker Hounds had no reason to exist; so we hear of them no more. It's sad how these traditions die out.

In spite of all, I still consider myself a Peewit.

Gordon Rendell

What it's About

The village of Hardington Mandeville lies at the very southern edge of Somerset, its parish boundary being also the county boundary with Dorset.

A lad, three years old when the war started in 1939, describes how he experienced the following six years.

With a father who was involved in engineering and agricultural contracting and a mother who was the head teacher at the local school, Gordon was often left to find his own amusement. Having an enquiring mind and time on his hands, he studied the village characters and was often caught up in their activities.

At the age of seven, he could be asked to cycle over to Farmer Gifford's to sort out his stationary engine – usually it was the float chamber full of hay seeds again, no problem!

Those were the days of paraffin lamps, cooking on a Primus stove or a black range, and a diet of bread and cheese, eggs and rabbit stew. Roast chicken was for a special occasion only, and sausages used to burst out of their skins.

The history of life in Hardington Mandeville in the 1940s might have been lost for ever if its events had not been stamped upon the mind of a little boy who, eighty years later, has brought the characters back to tell their own eccentric stories in the rhythmic dialect of Somerset. The stories are not only a history – they are great fun!

Angie Hodges

Setting the Scene

I was three years old when war was declared and at the time it didn't really register what was involved. The thing I remember most was my grandfather, my mother's father, making black-out panels for the garage windows. The garage, where Father repaired cars and did other sorts of engineering things, had a long window down the entire south wall. It was made, as many were in those days, of just vertical glazing bars filled in between with the used glass plates from the old plate cameras overlapping one another like weatherboarding. There were two windows on the north wall and a small one in the east end, through which you could see the time by the church clock across Court Close. The blackout frames were of 2″x1″ batten covered with a thick black cardboard and were

No 2 Engine.

religiously put in place at sunset, the time of which was shown in the newspapers of the day.

We had electricity provided by a Petter engine that chuffed away in a contented sort of manner as it did its job. I loved the smell of the hot oil as it mixed with the boiling water that jumped out of the big cooling tank every now and then. I did not much care for the smell of the chemical toilet that we had in those days, but it was luxury compared with some of the arrangements that other households in the village had. Up at the Manor Farm they had a "Two Holer" just off the front lawn which was arranged immediately over the stream that was actually the overflow from the horse pond, so they never had to "dig it and shift it." In actual fact it came on down the ditch past our front lawn, under the lane, and through the Rectory garden.

Talking of rectories, from 3 March 1934 until 2 July 1938 the rector was Richard James Hunt who drove a little black and green Morris. He was the last Rector to live in the old Rectory at the bottom of Rectory Lane, for when Robert Fitz-James Sawyer came

The Old Rectory.

Western Rectory.

in 1938, he lived in the new Rectory out near Hill End. He drove a maroon German Opel, which he soon got rid of when war broke out, after suffering the glares of his parishioners when he was seen driving this Teutonic piece of rubbish. Besides the Opel, there were five other cars in the village: Father had a black and green Austin twelve ALA784, Bob Turner at the Manor Farm had a black Hillman AMR286, Sonny White at the Royal Oak drove a black Vauxhall while Harold Curtis at the New Inn ran around in a black Morris and the Vickery family at Bridge Close Farm had a brown and beige Austin Sixteen GO9797.

Father, until 1939, was a chauffeur for the Johnson family, glove manufacturers, of Yeovil, until his boss, Ephraim Johnson died; then he bought a tractor and started agricultural contracting. Until then, everything was horse drawn and done quietly. We went into

Crewkerne to Gibbs's at Oxen Road and father bought this yellow Standard Fordson with a red spot. Where was the red spot you ask? It was a circle about 1½ " diameter on the differential casing, which indicated the gearing; an orange spot was higher geared and therefore faster though not having as much torque, or pulling power. It was delivered and Father drove it into the garage. Now I must tell you that at the time, my favourite colour was green; I was fanatical about it and I wanted Father to buy a green tractor, so while he was away working somewhere I found a pot of Brunswick green paint and an old brush and made a start on the offside front wheel. I painted about half of it and gave up. I can't remember why. Possibly I could see the task to paint all of it was too much to do before Father returned. Anyway I can remember him asking me why I had done it and I told him that I had wanted a green one. He drove it around for a bit with one wheel half painted green, I don't recall what the result was, whether it wore off or whether he got at it with some turps.

The War Agricultural Committee, "the War Ag" sent two ploughs, one was a Massey Harris, a nice green one, and the other a Cockshutt, a semi digger plough not at all suited to Hardington soil that was at best a thin layer on top of impenetrable clay. It was never used; it stood the whole of its life in the same place where it was unloaded. Then Father bought a Ransomes No. 9 long turnfurrow plough with three furrows, not two as were the others, but the third was not used as the tractor wasn't strong enough to pull three through Hardington's heavy soil. Eventually, in 1959 or thereabouts, I added the extra furrow and converted the plough to be hung on the hydraulic linkage of the Fordson Major that I used to drive at that time.

The first tractor FYB 141 soon had a mate, FYC 759, a green one, so Father had to find another driver for the second tractor. A big girl in the village, one Kathleen Purchase had tried her hand at the war effort in the Westland Aircraft factory and didn't like it much so approached Father for the job of tractor driver. She looked capable enough; some said she were "a mannish girt woman" and "built for the job," which she was.

Trying to keep in some sort of calendar order, my mother was headmistress at Hardington school and as a result I had a "Nanny", Jane Ransome, who looked after me while Mother was teaching. Ransome, was what I called her and we had a great time, we thought the world of each other. If I was in bed with a cold or something, I would call for her to come up to the bedroom and as soon as she looked around the door I would hurl my Teddy bear at her and she would throw it back. I remember its leg came off one day and the stuffing started coming out and poor Ransome had to repair it before mother came home.

The Evacuees

Then we had evacuees. They were delivered to Manor Farm and herded into the dairy where people from the village came to choose their allocated charges. I persuaded Mother to choose one Sally Hatch, a girl with pigtails and a green knitted hat. What's new? Green again! Mother grudgingly agreed and we took her home. What a jolt to the system! I had to share things and think of others. Still we didn't fight though I had difficulty in translating the broad East End dialect. She didn't stay with us long because her mother wanted her back with them because they were going "Hopping", which to me seemed a strange thing to be doing. Not realising that practically the whole of the East End of London went to Kent to help with gathering in the hop harvest and enjoying the open air for a couple of weeks' holiday and getting paid for it as well! There was no jumping about on one foot involved at all.

(L-R) on Horseback: Peggy Hatch (evacuee); John White; David Underhill (evacuee). Standing: Jean Lanham; Bronway Parry (evacuee); Norah Marsh; Keith Marsh. Jean Laughlin (neé Lanham).

The evacuees were a bit of a culture shock. Coming from the city, as they did, they had no idea at all as to the ways of the country and little respect for other people's property. John Field, who was staying at Struckmead Farm, opposite the Rectory, ran away and was eventually found several days later at "Pennels". This was a disused quarry on the south side of Hardington Moor that was currently being used as a landfill site for the local rubbish. We used to go there regularly; although we weren't supposed to, to look for pram wheels to make go-carts out of. We had to look out for an old chap who lived there in an evil smelling caravan; his job was to look after the site. He was called Bill Marsh, but we always called him "Gipsy Bill" and were always careful to see that he wasn't around when we went foraging. The old quarry was reputedly the source of the best roofing tiles anywhere, being used in the construction of the original Crewkerne School. John had built himself a sort of igloo construction out of old ammunition boxes and was living in there. Much later in life I heard that he had eloped with his girlfriend and gone to Gretna Green to be married by the blacksmith. Some evacuees fitted in quite well, to the extent that they didn't want to go back to London. Margaret Love stayed on and eventually married Bill Danes and lived in one of the Swedish houses at Hill End.

At about this time, we all assembled in the school where we were fitted out with gas masks; they smelled of rubber and after a couple of puffs you couldn't see out because the little window had steamed up. Later on we had to go back and have an additional filter taped on to the air inlet to cope with a different type of gas as well. Fortunately, we never needed to use them!

The Fleet Air Arm rented property in Hardington to house pilots from the Yeovilton Air Base and one of the cottages now called "Thatcher's Well," was in the High Street, next to "Carys." Its official address was 550 High Street, not that there were that many houses in the High Street, but it was a Lord Portman number. He used to number his houses in the order that they were built; 549 might be in Haselbury Plucknett and 551 in East Chinnock. Two other numbers I remember in Hardington were Barry House 336, and the centre one of the three at Rydons in Broadstone Lane where Rupert and Alice Giles lived. I thought that one was 332, but the number is no longer there now. I should remember it for I lived next door to it for five years in the western one of the three. Anyway, one Captain Sewell lived in 550 with his wife and they became very friendly with my parents. He used to fly a Spitfire and do the most hair-raising stunts with it. If he saw my mother coming home from school with an armful of books he would "Buzz" her, flying about twenty feet above her head. This was usually after he had been on some sortie or other and he would fly over Hardington to let his wife know he was OK. One day I was indoors at Rectory Cottage, where we lived down Rectory Lane. My mother and Alice Giles were outside, talking. Suddenly, they both started to scream as this Spitfire came down the lane, went past the window and shot vertically up in front of the beech trees at the bottom of the lane. I reached the window in time to see him rolling away back to Yeovilton. He came down that evening and apologised to mother for frightening her. It was said that he had been known to fly through the railway bridge at Hardington Marsh.

One day he and his wife asked if they could take me to the pictures to see *Snow White*, to which my parents agreed. I had never been to the cinema before and was absolutely enthralled; so much so that I insisted on seeing it again, telling Captain Sewell and his wife what was going to happen next. They had to explain to Mother why they had been gone so long. Later he left for a posting elsewhere and was replaced by Captain Blake who was much less fun. I heard that Captain Sewell was eventually killed in an air crash in Canada where he was training pilots. It appears that someone collided with him. Not his fault!

It was my fifth birthday and lo and behold what should turn up but a brand new green Fordson tractor, with the new clipped wings, GYA 24. It still had only three forward gears and a reverse with a brake that worked on the transmission, so you pushed the clutch pedal half-way down to operate the clutch and all the way down to put the brake on. There was also no hand brake; to hold the brake on, there was a hook on the floor that you located over the brake pedal. Even when they brought out the Fordson Major with independent brakes, it still had the same engine and gearbox.

Shortage of Rubber

In those days, because it was wartime and rubber was in short supply, all tractors were delivered with iron wheels to which you could bolt various attachments to give different amounts of grip depending on soil conditions. One such addition were "cleats" which were strips of angle iron that were bolted on to the flat surface diagonally. Then there were "grass lugs" that were little pyramid shapes for use on grassland in fine weather. Then there were "spade lugs" that were like large dragon's teeth about 5" long and used for ploughing. Of course, none of these could be used on the roads, especially in hot

Road bands.

weather or they would cause considerable damage, so we fitted "road bands". These were large iron hoops of flat metal about 6" wide that fitted over the spade lugs which kept them clear of the road surface; like the iron tyres on wooden waggon wheels, only much wider. The very nature of their design meant that grip was minimal on a steep hill. Talking of steep hills, Father was moving a pair of the aforesaid road bands to a tractor that had been working at East Coker, and had them lying on a large car trailer which we were towing behind the Austin. Going down Lodge Hill, which is quite steep, we heard a strange bell-like noise and were surprised to see one of the road bands passing us and going at ever increasing speed down the hill. The rope that was tying them on had frayed through. Fortunately, Lodge Hill has a sharp double bend in it and we watched as the errant object mounted the bank and disappeared through the hedge. Father stopped very gingerly as these things weighed about 2 to 3 cwt each and re-lashed the remaining road band. We continued to the bottom of the hill and turned left to see the offending escapee standing in the ditch, having burst through the hedge at the bottom of the field. These contraptions were the cause of other heart attacks in the area. Austin Whetham at Wicket's Beer Farm tried to go across the railway tracks and suffered the trauma of the smooth metal not being able to climb out of the space between the railway lines. He eventually got out by heaping ballast up to make a ramp. Not to be caught like that on a second occasion, he went across with spade lugs fitted and no road bands. This time the spade lugs dropped in between the check rails and jammed. He eventually let out the clutch with such a jolt that the tractor jumped in the air with fright and escaped minutes before the Exeter express came through.

The shortage of rubber was not only confined to tractor tyres, I remember lorries used for hauling hay would often have about three layers of canvas showing all the way round their tyres contributing to quite a number of punctures. During this time of change-over from horses to horse power one of the main contributors to punctures were cast off horse shoe nails in the roads and thorns in the fields. Father bought an air compressor (ex Westlands) to help him cope with the demand and also used it to sand blast sparking plugs and spray paint plus the ability to blow air into awkward places to remove dust and hayseeds.

By this time we had mowing machines, an Albion and a Bamlett for hay making and a Deering binder for cutting corn. So Stanley Hawkins, a local carpenter who lived down the moor at 6, St James' Terrace, next door to Ransome at number 7, was contracted to make two hay sweeps. These were like ten-pronged wooden forks about ten feet wide that fitted to the front axle of the tractor and used to sweep up the hay and push it to where they were building a hayrick. There the hay was made into a stack built on a "staddle" consisting of a base made of timber faggots to keep the hay off the ground and prevent it from going rotten. Some farmers had the luxury of an elevator, some of these powered by a horse walking round and around a geared capstan or the more up to date ones having a petrol engine which provided motive power. As long as the hay remained dry they kept going until it was too dark to see, having no lights on the tractor. Sometimes one could only tell where

The Old Post Office.

the hayrick was by the glow of the cigarettes smoked by the men waiting for the next sweepful.

When the rick was finished it resembled the shape of a house. Then Joe Legg, who lived at the Post Office, telephone number West Coker 359, (now "Midway,") and had a few cows, would come along and thatch it to keep the rain out. He used reed that the farmer had saved from last year's wheat harvest, oat straw at a pinch, and held it in place with wooden spars that he made from branches he cut from his willow trees lining the ditch. He used to spend many winter evenings splitting, sharpening and bending willow in the old cottage adjoining the Post Office. The aroma was absolutely delightful. He sat on an old chair with a section of old car tyre clipped onto his right knee as a guard and a very sharp bill hook that he cut himself with occasionally, but not seriously thankfully.

He and his wife had an evacuee, Brian Tiernan from Balham who was my best friend and some say the spitting image of me, as on many occasions I had been seen where I was not. We used to do everything together, the favourite being making camps in the woods and copses where we sat and tried to smoke dead nettle stems with binder twine pushed up the hollow centre. It tasted foul and we burnt our lips and tongues. Another occupation was "tracking". After school a gang of us would split in two and one party would set off running and with a piece of chalk would mark arrows on the road surface when we came to a road junction. At the junction of Barry Lane and Ridgeway Lane there used to be kept a large pile of chippings for resurfacing the road. Sometimes we found quartz amongst it and pretended the pieces were diamonds and we treasured them greatly. When they were re-surfacing the roads, the steam roller would be parked there over night. It resembled a sleeping dragon, for its tarpaulin curtains around the cab were drawn closed and it was still extremely hot and made burbling noises and dripped hot water. We didn't stand too close in case it blew up. We ran miles and during the holidays when there was a meet of the Cattistock Hunt we would follow them for hours. No one seemed to worry that we didn't come home until nearly tea time having been given lunch at Hardington Marsh by Gladys Rawlings who had felt sorry for these mud–spattered urchins. Straight into the bath when I got back; I can still remember how those bramble scratches stung in the hot water.

Summers in those days seemed to be perfect, until the Americans arrived. I noticed that a day started off sunny and bright until the high flying B17 Flying Fortresses made vapour trails that by late morning had spread sufficiently to cover the whole sky and make the day become overcast. I was reminded of this when the Icelandic volcano Eyjafallajokull erupted and the airlines were grounded in case they got ash in their engines. We had beautiful weather, and I believe the pollution caused by the volcano was less than that caused by the aircraft that would normally have been flying.

Joe Legg didn't have much land for his few cows, only the orchard, so he rented some: Court Close, adjoining his property and North Field, found down over North Lane and then left by Millcombe Pond and out through a muddy unpaved bridleway; both fields now belong to my son Ivan and me. Joe also rented some rough land down by Hardington Marsh. To get to it we went up over the High Street and almost straight across The Ridgeway to go down Common Lane. Joe acquired an old Morris car with a noisy back axle that sounded like the car they used to use on the Archer's programme on the B.B.C., and he used to drive this car all the way down Common Lane to the fields at the bottom that were full of thorn bushes and an ideal place for Whitethroat nests. The lane was barely wide enough for the car to get through and if it was a bit wet and muddy, Joe really used to attack the steep parts on the way back up to a frightening degree, with wheels spinning and us lads bouncing up and down in the back along with the empty buckets.

Parsnip Wine

That reminds me of the time I was riding in the back of Father's car with a lot of bottles. Sometime before this, Father had been over to West Coker to collect Mother and me from a visit to Auntie Addie. Granddad was sampling some parsnip wine that he had made and offered Father a taste. Father naively thinking it was non-alcoholic had half a pint. He said it was very nice and was encouraged to indulge in a second helping. They eventually left with numerous bottles on the back seat of the car. Having been made to sign the pledge when he was engaged in his chauffeuring capacity, he was not used to alcohol and he drove off the road completely on two occasions on the way home and spent most of the next day in bed. He removed the bottles from the car when he felt up to it and put them on a shelf in the outhouse until such time that he could decide what to do with them.

During the war, Father's garage was very much like a working men's club where several of his friends would spend an evening watching father working on a car or something. I think it helped that he kept a tin of tobacco on a shelf over the bench. He said it kept the customers there longer. Father used to smoke a little but gave it up on finding that the Rector, Rev. Morgan Beddoe, who used to cadge cigarettes from him, never returned them. In the winter there was a coke-burning Tortoise stove keeping the place nice and snug and with the black-out panels up at the windows they could discuss the world in general for as long as they liked. Arthur Adams would come in from next door, Ern' Hawkins from Coker Hill and one or two of the bell ringers like Doug' Ransome and Fred Marsh. Arthur would head for the bench as soon as he came in, reach up to the shelf for the tin without looking and fill his pipe; then carefully replacing the lid he would put the tin back on the shelf. Then he would take several seconds to light his pipe, pressing the burning tobacco down into the bowl and making sure it was drawing properly. Come to think of it, it was the only time I ever heard Arthur stop talking, he seemed to chatter on unceasingly. Perhaps being of Welsh descent had something to do with it? Various other gents would arrive during the evening and warm themselves in front of the stove and chat away aimlessly until they thought their wives would be missing them by now, whereon they would quietly melt away. They probably felt safer there, as there was the inspection pit that they could use as an air-raid shelter if the need arose. One night Arthur wasn't the first there and while he was going through his ritual one of the others said,

"Bert, if only you had some drink here, you'd put Harold Curtis out of business." Harold Curtis was the landlord of the New Inn. He was also a farmer who let me ride on the back of Tony, his horse and also the bull occasionally, but only when it was on a lead. Both the pubs in Hardington were farms as well. This gave Father an idea as how to dispose of the parsnip wine. He certainly wasn't going to drink it and it seemed a shame to pour it away.

"I think that can be arranged," he said and fetched a bottle from the shelf in the outhouse, plus some mugs from indoors.

The bottle saw them through the evening and in reply to the query as to whether there were any more, Father said that there were, but they would only come out on special occasions. It was surprising how many occasions were suggested as special enough to open another bottle and they started calling on Sunday mornings when Father was back from church.

Incendiaries

One Sunday morning the usual gang of regulars had arrived plus Austin Whetham who told Father that a German bomber had been trying to find the Westland Aircraft factory the night before and had been chased by a couple of Seafires from Yeovilton. To save weight and thus increase speed he had jettisoned his load of incendiary bombs over Penn Wood. Apparently one had come through the thatched roof of Wicket's Beer farmhouse and had been put out with a bucket of water and another had landed on a hayrick by the railway cottages at Whistle Bridge. Father, being the local sergeant in the Special Constabulary, had to investigate, so off we went with a couple of cardboard boxes in the back of the car. When we reached the bottom of Rectory Hill at Pendomer we could see a couple of burnt-out lumps of metal on the milk stand and as we went further there were incendiary bombs hanging up in the branches like icicle decorations on a Christmas Tree. They shone in the sunlight, being made of silvery magnesium and they swayed in the breeze being caught by their tail fins. They looked quite pretty. Then every so often, one would detach itself and drop to the ground with a great bang, a bright flare of flame and a cloud of white smoke. We were very careful to avoid standing beneath one. In some places the ground was quite soft and several hadn't exploded so Father collected these and put them in the cardboard boxes in the back of the car. These we took home, leaving a notice warning people to stay out of the area. In the six months following this event, Bert Whetham at Bryant's Farm said that he lost seven cows to magnesium poisoning. When we arrived home, Father rang the police who said they would get the bomb squad out there to make it all safe.

Meanwhile, out in the garage the chaps were inspecting one of the bombs and wondering how it worked. They'd put it in the vice and were trying to unscrew it. Father soon put a stop to that, suggesting that it might be booby-trapped, and produced a hammer and chisel to cut off the rivets securing the tail fin. He then took a breast drill out of a drawer and proceeded to drill a half inch hole in the rear end which resulted in some grey powder flowing out. This was caught on some brown paper used for making gaskets. The bomb was now considered safe. At this point someone suggested that this might be one of those special occasions so Father went to fetch another bottle.

Eli Taylor

While Father was fetching the bottle, Eli Taylor turned up on his 1928 AJS Motorcycle with the hand gear change on the right hand side of the tank and the lever throttle on the handlebars. He had come for some carbide for his acetylene lamps and a drop of Pool petrol. He wore a very heavy, dark blue great coat that looked as though it could have belonged to a bus driver and a peaked cap with a press stud at the front to hold the front down on to the peak. When motorcycling, the cap was turned around back to front so that the peak didn't interfere with the goggles that were made of leather, trimmed with dark brown rabbit fur. Father reappeared with a bottle. Chain grips were utilised next to unscrew the flat nose of the bomb and the contents removed to reveal a 40mm nail with a large aluminium head similar to a drawing pin; beneath which was a light spring, just sufficiently strong to support the pin. Beneath this was an aluminium disk about the size of a 10p coin with a raised centre incorporating a shiny blue disk about 5mm across; It was deduced that when the bomb hit the ground, the pin would carry on under its own momentum and pierce this thing that was probably a primer or detonator. Eli hadn't tasted parsnip wine before and was remarking how nice it was while I was trying to see what this disc thing was like that they were talking about. I didn't get a chance to study it at length because Doug Ransome placed it on the vice and hit it with a hammer. God what a bang! For a long time afterwards I could see people's mouths moving but I couldn't hear what they were saying. My ears were going Zing, Zing, Zing.

Eli jumped straight up about six inches. If he hadn't had such a heavy coat he could probably have managed nine. This caused him to spill the drop of wine he had left in the mug so he reached for the bottle to put things right and he needed another drop after that because he was still shaking. While he was readjusting his nerves, the gang went home to dinner and Father filled Eli's bike with petrol, took the money and the coupons and fetched the carbide. It, the carbide, was sold in black and yellow tins twice as high as a cocoa tin but not quite as fat. Eli decided that he'd had enough excitement and would go home for his dinner; he now turned his cap around and put on his pair of goggles and started his machine, after carefully "tickling the carburettor" until petrol was seen to squirt out of a little hole in the top of the float chamber. We heard him chug up the lane and turn left while we went in for our roast beef and Yorkshire pudding. It seems that Eli was no more used to Grandfather's parsnip wine than Father was and when his wife, Bessie came to look for him at half past three because he hadn't come home for his dinner she found him fast asleep on the bank just around the corner at the top of Rectory Lane amongst the celandines, cuddling his motor cycle. She wasn't pleased. When she did manage to wake him, all he would say was,

"What a bloody bang!"

Father fetched his bike back and put it in the garage for him to collect on Monday.

Eli had an interesting outlook on life. He had a few cows that were more like pets. He didn't tie them up for milking like other farmers. His cow stall more closely resembled a garage, just a square, rendered room with a single light bulb hanging from a couple of feet of flex from the centre of the ceiling. Eli sat on a three-legged milking stool in the middle of this room with a bucket between his knees and a cow would walk in and stand in front of him to be milked, then the cow, deciding that it was empty, would walk away and another, under its own volition would replace it. They all had names of course.

"This is Christmas" announced Eli, " 'cos that's when her was born."

He was a complete opposite to Douglas Foot of Hewingbere Farm down at Hardington Marsh. Douglas was educated at Sherborne and used to listen to "Today in Parliament" on the radio. He had a big farm with hayricks in abundance and maintained a large herd of red Devon cows. His policy was,

"If we have a bad summer and don't make any hay, the Lord will follow it with a winter so mild that we sha'nt need it." Whilst Eli prophesied,

"If we have a poor summer and only make bad hay, the Lord will send a winter so hard that the cows will be glad to eat anything!"

Doc Brown

Eli and Betty had a neighbour, Doctor Brown; I don't know why he was called doctor, or more commonly Doc. I believe he was educated at Beaminster Grammar school in Dorset and occasionally would stand on his bed and recite great tracts of Shakespeare. You will gather from that fact alone that he was perhaps slightly unusual. I was given to understand that he had the misfortune, sometime during the 1914-1918 war to be hit in the head with a piece of shrapnel; they repaired his skull with a silver plate which he subsequently carried for the rest of his life and although it did not seem to have any adverse effect most of the time, he was known to behave somewhat irrationally at the time of the new moon.

He lived on the west side of Partway Lane just up the road from Eli and Betty, in a wooden shack like a large chicken house, which he used to add on to occasionally with bits of old galvanised iron sheeting; access to it was by a plank across the roadside ditch. On one of his monthly diversions, he papered the whole of the outside of it with pages from the *Picture Post* magazine. On the sides that didn't get too much weather it stayed like it for years. Eli's sister Gertie used to try to keep an eye on him as best as she could.

He used to do seasonal farm work for Percy Lock who had a threshing machine. His usual job was to feed the sheaves of corn into the thresher. We, as children used to love the thresher coming to Manor Farm as the rick yard was right against the school wall and we could see most of the thresher above it. Manoeuvring the thing into position and levelling it took some time and then the tractor had to be positioned just right and a huge flat belt to transmit the power from the pulley on the tractor was crossed, like a figure of eight and slid over the pulley on the thresher. The tractor, a huge American International Harvester W9, was moved backwards until the belt was tight, then the brakes applied and the wheels chocked; then the exciting part. The clutch on the tractor was slowly released and the belt started to move. The straw walkers at the top of the machine that spewed the threshed straw out of the machine into the baler came to life. Silently at first, then as the clutch was fully engaged the throttle was slowly opened. A low murmur was heard from somewhere inside the monster, which increased in volume and pitch until the thresher was working at its designed speed. The sound now coming from the beast was a loud hum with an attendant rocking and shaking to the rhythm of the straw walkers. The sound was an harmonic one, with the sound being generated by the revolving drum beating the grain out of the ears of corn and the winnowing fan, blowing dust and chaff out of the bottom of the machine. There was very little concentration on lessons while the threshing machine was working. High upon the top of the machine was where Doc used to work. His job was to feed the sheaves of corn head first into the threshing drum, first cutting the strings with a knife made out of an old triangular mowing machine knife section attached to a wooden handle that had a string loop to go around his wrist so that he couldn't drop it into the works. It was continuous work, hot and dusty and being bent over all of the time was hard on the back. There were usually two men on the corn rick with pitchforks tossing the sheaves one at a time onto the top of the thresher for Doc to deal with, where Doc would take them, turn them the right way round, if the feeder was careless, inconsiderate, or just downright awkward and then with a suitable expletive, would feed them evenly into the drum. At this point the machine made a satisfying groan, rather like a chef sampling a particularly tasty dish. This continued from breakfast until lunchtime with a frequent swig of cider and then the machine was allowed to go back to sleep for an hour while everyone had their bread and cheese or sandwiches. Everyone that is except Doc, he just had cider. I never saw him eat anything; I don't suppose he could be bothered to prepare anything for his lunch.

At two o' clock they raised the monster from its slumber by re-starting the tractor and he roared into life again. The two lads pitching up the sheaves decided to torment Doc and gradually started to speed up; he speeded up a little to try to catch up but the sheaves came quicker still. In an effort to catch up, he started to throw the sheaves into the drum without bothering to cut the strings, but the thresher didn't care for this treatment and started to complain, loudly. But it didn't have to put up with it for very long as Doc was being buried under the avalanche of sheaves and was spending all his time trying to climb on top of them. Percy was checking the grain running into the bags at the front of the machine when two sheaves fell on his head and he soon put a stop to that nonsense.

Percy bought a second machine which was a Reed Comber. At first sight you might think they were identical, but instead of the sheaves being fed directly into a central drum, they were fed in horizontally, still at the top of the machine, between two moving belts with the ears on the left. As they were fed in between the belts in an even and thinly spread line, they passed a drum with long fingers rotating at high speed which knocked the ears off the stalks allowing them to thus fall into the threshing drum beneath, while the headless and now combed straw continued to the far end of the machine where it slid down a sloping ramp into a trusser that tied it into large bundles ready for use for thatching roofs, hay ricks or even more straw ricks.

One of the events associated with thatching was rat catching. Straw ricks always had at least one family of rats living in the staddle and living off the grain, so often a wire netting fence was erected around the area and a terrier or two allowed access. Percy's son, Ivan, used to have a terrier that went with him and used to sleep on the tractor seat for most of the time, but when the fence was erected as the stack was significantly reduced in height, he sat up and took notice, squealing in anticipation of what was to come; he knew that the rats and mice would soon be evacuating their homes in the stack and bolting for cover elsewhere. He moved like lightning, a quick nip and a squeak and he was poised alert watching for the next one. I don't know what his record was for a day, but I do know that Ivan said that he'd killed sixty four rats out of one straw rick.

There was always the unexpected. Kathleen, who worked for my Father was pitching up sheaves at Charlie Gifford's at Haselbury

Park Farm onto George Mitchell's thresher when a mouse ran up the inside of the leg of her overalls. You've never heard such a noise, and not from the mouse. Her screams were louder than the whistle on George's traction engine that was powering the thresher. She was hysterical, and didn't know what to do for the best; being the only female amongst a crowd of men and of a somewhat reserved disposition. She didn't want to remove her trousers, neither did she want the mouse inside of them. The men couldn't have helped even if they had been asked, for they were all helpless with laughter. The mouse, unable to stand the noise that Kathleen was making, left by the other trouser leg in a quest for somewhere quieter. She then tucked her trouser legs inside her socks to prevent any further rodental activity. Unlike another fellow on another occasion who had a rat run up his trouser leg. He grabbed the bulge in his trousers with both hands when it was half-way up his inner thigh and held on until his mates could remove his trousers. When they eventually removed the garment they found the rat dead, he had squeezed it to death. I must explain that George Mitchell's threshing machine was towed to its destination by a traction engine and then powered by it when on station. I actually worked with it on one occasion just before he changed it for a Field Marshall tractor, much less spectacular. It had a single horizontal cylinder diesel engine that produced a most distinctive "Plonk – Plonk" exhaust note and was started with either a piece of smouldering paper and a starting handle or a cartridge, like a twelve-bore shotgun cartridge but without the lead shot in it. The traction engine powered outfit was later seen in the film *Far From the Madding Crowd*.

Another job that Doc did at harvest time was following the binder and "stitching up", or "stooking" the sheaves of corn. This involved standing eight or ten sheaves on their butt ends and leaning against one another so that the breeze could blow through and dry them before being loaded onto waggons and then built into ricks. I remember oat straw had to stay out for two Sundays, but wheat straw could be carried with the water running out of it. We, as kids, used to love hiding in these, suffering the inevitable stubble-scratched knees in the process.

On this particular occasion, it was in the middle of August during the school summer holidays and the sun was hot and prickly; it was so hot that the tar on the roads was bubbling and you could hear the bubbles popping. We used to poke them because they were nice and squidgy, but we inevitably poked too hard and eventually burst them getting hot tar on our fingers that always somehow seemed to get on our clothes. We wandered into a cornfield on Court Dairy Farm at East Chinnock belonging to the Corbett family where Doc and several others were stitching up the freshly-bound sheaves and Doc was wearing Wellington boots and appeared to be making heavy going of it. To us it seemed a most unsuitable footwear for all this heat, but us boys didn't consider that it might be his only footwear and to draw attention to it might cause embarrassment. Piers, whose father's farm it was went straight up to him and said

"Aren't your feet hot in those boots?"

"No, boy," came the reply, "I've got 'em full of water and when that gets warm I go down to the river and change it."

Another time I saw him wearing Wellingtons, he was cleaning out the ditch outside his hut. Rupert Giles, who used to work for my father, stopped to speak to him as we came up the lane and noticed that the toes were split and letting water in.

"Those boots aren't much good Doc, they're letting the water in."

"Don't matter" said Doc, standing on one leg and holding the other one out horizontally in front of him.

"I've cut holes in the heels to let it out; look!" He had, the water was pouring out.

It was strange how the moon seemed to affect him. He had an elderly bicycle as his means of transport and come the time of the month he would cycle to Haselbury or North Perrott and jump out in front of ladies in the dark. Most of them knew him and told him to go home, which probably deflated his ego, but one evening he went too far and was chased by a farmer with a shotgun so he ran home. In the morning he had no memory of the event , but wondered where his bike was. Strangely, come the next new moon, he walked back to North Perrott and collected it from the ditch where he had left it. His bicycle was quite well-known, especially to the local constabulary with the mudguards and carrier tied on with binder twine. He was found by the Dorset police at about two o' clock one morning on his way to Dorchester to post his football coupon. They kindly brought him and his bike back to the county border at Closworth and pointed him towards Yeovil. His bike was to be his downfall eventually, but not before he had made a nuisance of himself on several other occasions. One night he went into the Yeovil Police Station at Petter's Way and "chatted up" a young policewoman who was on duty at the enquiry desk. She was quite safe, being behind a glass screen with a six inch hole in the centre for conversation with an enquiree. Not having much to do, she tolerated his incoherent ramblings for some time before she managed to get rid of him. He hadn't been gone five minutes before he was back with a big bunch of daffodils.

"You've been so kind to me my dear, I've brought you some flowers." He had, bulbs, dirt, the lot. He forced them through the hole in the glass dropping dirt all over the paperwork on her desk. In the morning, it was quite clear from whence they had come; there was a gap in the flowerbed of the police house next door. Anyway, his final act of remembrance was when he tried to take his bicycle through the revolving glass doors of the Three Choughs Hotel in Hendford and broke two panes of heavily engraved glass.

Unfortunately the police were called in officially and I never saw him with a bike after that.

He was obviously a character who had gained the sympathy of the Parish Council, because when his shack blew away during a gale, making him virtually homeless, they bought and presented him with a brand new chicken house to live in, though it never quite looked the part without the pages from the *Picture Post* magazine. It is no longer there.

Bomb Disposal

Mentioning the police, do you remember the bomb?

Well, we kept the bomb as a door stop for years until the seventies or eighties when I heard on the news that these things after a period of time were prone to self-combusting, so one evening I took it into Yeovil Police Station, where there was a young WPC on duty behind the glass screen who reversed smartly to the other side of the room when I stood it on the counter.

"What's that?" she said. A little trace of uncertainty was revealing itself in her manner.

"A World War 2 incendiary bomb." I explained.

"Will it go off?" She showed genuine concern.

"No." I reassured her, "It's quite safe. If you could have seen what it's gone through you wouldn't ask that question."

"Why have you brought it here?" she queried.

"To give it to you." I said.

"Why?" She obviously didn't get the point.

"I understand they have a habit of going off on their own account and I wanted to get rid of it before it does." This didn't seem to calm the situation at all.

"What am I going to do with it?/" She enquired.

" I should find someone else and give it to them." I suggested and turned to leave.

"You can't just leave it there. You'll have to fill out a form." And she sidled past it to get to a filing cabinet which failed to produce a form for the acceptance of weapons, German or otherwise.

"This will have to do." She said. "It's a form for handing in stray dogs and cats."

Question 1, Type	A, Bomb
Question 2, Breed.	A, Incendiary
Question 3, Colour.	A, Silver/grey
Question 4, Height	A, 15"
Question 5, Distinguishing marks	A, Swastika and black tail fin
Question 6, Age approx.	A, 35 years
Question 7, Value.	A, Scrap
Question 8, Where found.	A, Pendomer woods
Question 9, When found.	A, 1942 (year not time)

I left, with the bomb still standing to attention on the counter. I don't know; you try to do the right thing. Still, I might have been done for carrying an offensive weapon, had I found a less sympathetic officer.

Busted Half Shaft

The last bottle of wine was brought out on D Day. Father appeared a little disappointed. He apologised.

"It's the last one" he said, "and the cork must have blown out. I'll have to throw it away." The top inch of wine was solid with the bodies of drowned flies.

"No, Don't do that," shouts Arthur. "Let's have a bit of rag and we'll strain they out." A piece of not too oily rag was found and the wine ceremoniously decanted into the mugs. It was decided that as the bottle could not be re-corked it had better be consumed.

"Nothing wrong with it." pronounced Arthur. "Yers to Victory."

"To Victory," was the unanimous reply.

Until I started school I went nearly everywhere with Father. Charles Dye & Co., the motor factors, were quite interesting, going into the store room looking at bolts, belts, gears and cables as was Hill Sawtell the ironmongers with all their lovely tools and fittings. There were three other ironmongers in Yeovil at that time: Neal & Williams and Higdons, both in Middle Street and Cannons in Westminster Street. F.W. Sibley's of Goldcroft were heavy engineers and had beautiful heavy machinery, as did Fred Dibble in Reckleford. He, Fred, had a one-eyed engineer called Ted, who used to come out to us when father had an engine that needed the cylinders re-boring. He would bring out a machine that did the job in situ. My least interesting place was the Midland Bank in the Borough. I thought that to be the most boring. Another interesting place was Crowthers in Beer Street, he was a very clever engineer who invented a machine that turned calf skin into pig skin which was a much more expensive commodity. This machine was like a huge mangle, similar to the one we had at home to squeeze the water out of the washing, only the rollers weren't wooden, they were brass. One roller had thousands of tiny little pins sticking up all over its surface, something like the drum of a musical box, while its mate had a tiny little hole to accept each pin and when a skin was passed through the rollers, it came out the other side with thousands of little pores just like a pig skin. The next time you see some pig skin gloves take a closer look.

On one occasion when we were visiting Crowther's, Adolf decided that he would try to bomb Westlands and there were a couple of nearby bangs with a bit of a bump and the building twitched and a little window fell out. The next thing we heard was the sound of a couple of fighters roaring past to sort out the bomber that had caused the disturbance.

On another occasion, Thursday 12 August 1943, when we came to leave, Father started the engine and engaged bottom gear, let out the clutch, then, nothing. He checked one or two things but we still didn't move.

"Hop out son and have a look underneath to see if the prop' shaft is going round."

"Yes, he is Dad; lovely and fast."

"Half shaft has gone. We'll have to go and see Len Bollen."

Len Bollen had the garage in Huish, opposite the Bee Hive Inn. Not a long walk, just up over Orchard Street and turn right. When we arrived there were four workmen with tyre levers kneeling around a clutch plate on the floor. They were trying to compress a huge central spring so that a fifth member could insert a pin or something to hold it in place.

"Go on! A bit more! Nearly there!" came the encouraging cries, when "TWANG", the five men were left looking at the space where the spring had been. Above their heads came a bang as it hit the underside of the galvanised corrugated iron roof then a series of "Blings" and "Blangs" as it made its way around the workshop amongst the other cars and equipment. Len appeared out of the office to see what all the noise was about. He was shortish and fairly stout with black, curly hair looking slightly Italian, and when he had finished giving character references to the workmen, he enquired as to the reason for our visit. Father explained we had a broken half shaft and needed a tow home, so Len instructed one of his staff to see to it. Len had a huge American Packard 8, more than capable of the job, so it was decided that it would be best to go via West Coker and down over Coker Hill, rather than up Primrose Hill and Pig Hill from Hardington Moor. So off we set up over Hendford Hill and along the West Coker Road and past White post. Whether Len's driver had forgotten he was towing us, or had no previous experience of same, I don't know, but we were doing fifty and there was this bump and a scraping noise and Father had his hand on the horn button. The Austin had a klaxon horn and it sounded like a U Boat when it came to "Dive, Dive, Dive." The car had also taken up a peculiar angle where we were looking up in the air. The Packard eventually stopped in a cloud of smoke, (Len couldn't get replacement piston rings for it) our offside rear wheel had come off and we had left a gouge mark in the road caused by the back plate coming in contact with the road. A motorist who had been going in the opposite direction had stopped and was wheeling our lost wheel with its brake drum and bit of half shaft still attached, towards us.

"Is this yours?" he said. What a damn fool question. So I then had to wait, sitting on the bank on the side of the road to make sure no one stole anything, while Len's driver went back to Huish with Father to get the towing ambulance which looked like two wheels at the end of a long pole which went under the back axle to raise the car off the ground. While they were away somebody stopped their car and looked at me accusingly as though I had caused the accident then drove on. Father and Len's man returned then with the back axle up on the ambulance and the steering wheel lashed, the car was towed backwards to Hardington.

Friday 13th

Well, the following day was Friday 13th; and an unluckier day we have never experienced. It was during the school holidays, otherwise I wouldn't have been there. It was in the middle of the harvesting season and Father, with Kath was cutting corn for Farmer Lucas on the West Coker ridge. They had finished one field and had to pack the binder up into its transporting mode to travel up the lane between the two fields. You had to jack it up, fit its road wheels and move the drawbar and half dismantle the fan; you actually towed it sideways on the road because it was narrower in that position. They decided to move to the next field and then stop for a bite to eat as it was mid-day.

As the lane was extremely rough they decided that the grass lugs fitted would not damage the road surface so made their way to the next gateway up the lane and turned in. The field was of grass, very steep, with a large quantity of gorse in the top western area. I was at the bottom of the field having been exploring as the tractor and binder started down. It started to pick up speed and I saw father waving at me and shouting something that I couldn't hear, so I started in his direction. I could see that one of the driving wheels had started going backwards and the grass lugs throwing up fountains of bits of turf. Suddenly the front wheels jerked sharply to the right and the steering wheel was twisted out of Father's hands and over the whole lot went. I have often wondered since, if I was the cause of the tractor turning over, because if Father had been holding the steering wheel with both hands, would he have been able to keep it going straight? I can't remember if it rolled more than once, but it finished upside down with Father underneath. Kath was screaming and running down the field; she had been closing the gate. I started to run up the hill towards the mess to see Kath trying to push the tractor over. She shouted at me,

"Go and get Mr White, he's in the field across the lane." I ran as fast as I could to the top of the field, down the lane to a gateway on the other side of the lane where I saw a group of men sitting down having their lunch.

"Which of you is Mr White?" I asked.

"I am," said one of them.

"The tractor's turned over on top of Dad." Didn't they run? I couldn't keep up with them, and when I arrived at the scene they were pushing the tractor off of Dad. Then one of them ran to Lucas's Farm, whose field it was to phone for an ambulance. They must have rung Mother as well, because the next thing I remember was Mother appearing through a hedge and over a barbed wire fence. I thought this quite unusual at the time because I'd never seen Mother climb through a hedge or go over a barbed wire fence. While she was coming up the field I picked up the hitch pin that attached the binder to the tractor; it was bent. I held it out to show Father but he didn't seem interested. Mother then arrived completely out of breath to see Father sitting up supported by two of Mr White's workmen and Kath about to give him a cup of tea. Mother smacked the cup out of her hand and I heard her say.

"You don't give anything to drink to someone who's going to hospital." Then I heard the bell of the ambulance as it came up the lane. Things were a bit of a blur after that. Father was taken off to Yeovil General Hospital and Mother and I followed in someone's car. Then later we were taken home. Father spent a couple of days in Yeovil before being moved to Exminster in Devon where the government had taken over one wing of an enormous mental hospital for serious bone cases, mainly wounded servicemen. We rode with him in the ambulance. It wasn't a very comfortable ride for Father and on the way I remember we stopped outside a little cottage for one of the ambulance men to go in a fetch Father a cup of water. It was a long journey and what seemed an even longer wait when we arrived at this huge Victorian brick-built hospital with its quarter mile tulip-lined drive from the lodge gates. I don't remember how we got home again, but get home we did and we used to go to visit Father every Saturday by train from Yeovil Junction to Exeter Central and then by bus to Exminster. When they had examined him thoroughly there, they discovered that he had a broken back, two broken ribs, a punctured lung and a broken collar bone. His back, which had started to heal out of alignment, had to be broken again and he was put in a plaster jacket from his neck down to his hips. This resulted in a plaster sore in the middle of his back which they attended to by cutting a little window in the jacket so that they could treat the area. He was in this jacket for about six months, I think. My time scale and order of events may be a little vague after seventy years, but I do remember walking up the long drive from the main road as the air-raid siren sounded over Exeter and one of the inmates from the mental wing was slashing at the tulips in the beds by the side of the drive, shouting,

"Lie down you buggers, take cover. Hitler's coming," while another was lighting a cigarette with a magnifying glass, as they weren't allowed matches.

All of this time mother not only continued with her teaching but ran the agricultural contracting business as well. In retrospect I really don't know how she did it, but it was war time and people just got on with it.

After the Accident

With Father out of the way, the iron road bands were too heavy for Kathleen to manage so Mother had Stan Hawkins, the chap who made our two hay sweeps, make some wooden ones like the fellows of a wagon wheel that were in four sections and fitted in between the spade lugs. These were bolted in place and were shod with sections of car tyre to protect the wooden surface and also give a bit of grip. The other advantage was that you didn't need a jack to fit them. You just fitted a couple to each wheel and then drove on a couple of yards and then fitted the others. I would watch Stan working away with a lump of wood and a couple of sawing horses, (low wooden trestles) and marvelled at how shiny and sharp his tools were. He would beaver away with a cigarette between his lips and his fair to ginger curly hair full of little wood chips. The cigarette never left his lips and he would tilt his head every now and again when the smoke went in his eye. He never wasted any tobacco, for he smoked the cigarette right down to the end, blowing out the last quarter inch of tobacco leaving just a little ring of paper between his lips. Why did he never burn himself? Later, Father bought a '34 black and blue Austin Six YD2986 which he proceeded to cut the body off and turn into a pick-up for carrying TVO (tractor vaporising oil) out to the fields. Stan then had to make a wooden windscreen frame for it. I don't know where Stan found the time to do all these jobs, because he was a full time chippy at Shillabeere's, building firm, in Yeovil. Stan had a son called Terry with whom I used to play and I always liked going down to the moor to his place after school because his mum used to make us egg and chips with Chef tomato ketchup. Why are all these products that used to be so tasty now unavailable, like McConockie's Pan Yan Pickle and Eiffel Tower lemonade crystals, to name just three?

This vehicle, now christened "the Jeep" did sterling work carrying fuel and spares to the tractors where they were working. It had wire wheels (spoked), like Father's car, and at that time Harold Curtis at the New Inn kept geese amongst other farmyard stock and the old white gander took offence at the Jeep going by the yard gate and used to come flying out to chase it and peck at the tyres. One morning he misjudged it and got his head stuck between the spokes of the front wheel. By the time we had stopped he had done several revolutions in a rather undignified manner. Surprisingly he survived, twisting his head back out of the spokes he staggered back to the yard making hoarse honking noises. He never chased us again. Instead, he shouted defiantly from the yard entrance as we went by.

We had a similar incident once going down over Bridge Close Hill. Opposite the entrance to Bridge Close Farm is a gateway into the orchard, where the chicken used to like scratching about. Mr Vickery kept corn and other feed in a building on the north side of the yard with the door in full view of the gate. If the chicken saw him go in they all shot across the road from the orchard to the yard in case they were in for a treat. On this occasion they got more than a treat, for Mr Vickery went into the meal house just as we were bundling down the road with a load of fuel. We, and the chicken, arrived at the gate at the same time. There were feathers everywhere and when I looked back, expecting to see dead chicken all over the road there was not one casualty. Apart from a few feathers still blowing around, the road was clear.

Being the only man in the house while Father was in hospital, I was occasionally called on to do jobs you wouldn't normally expect a seven year old to be doing. Charlie Gifford from Haselbury Park Farm was known to ring up and complain that his Lister engine that was used to pump water up to the farm had stopped. I had been with Father many times on his trips to get Charlie's engine going and knew what the most likely problem was. Hay seeds in the float chamber. So with a few spanners and a screwdriver in the saddlebag on my bicycle I would pedal off and sort it out. I had to get Charlie in to turn it over when I had finished as I wasn't strong enough to pull it over compression, but he didn't mind that when it chugged into life and water started flowing again. I was rewarded with a glass of lemonade by his daughter, Betty.

Most of the farmers in that area were Father's customers. As well as Charlie Gifford at Haselbury Park Farm, there were the

Oxenburys at Whitevine, the Buddens at Kingswood, Farmer Dare at Downclose and Lindsey Burton at Grey Abbey, the North Perrott Fruit Farm on occasions and Farmer Smith, whose son Gordon I eventually went to school with at Crewkerne. Then there were the farmers Ebbs and Neil in Haselbury, Gerald Thorne at East Lease and the Matravers at Moultons. That was a place to go to!

Foreign Aid

Ernie and Flossie Matravers lived at Moultons Farm between Hardington Marsh and North Perrott, sharing the same boundary as the Foots at Hewingbere Farm. The farm house was small, stone built and thatched with the minimum of facilities. No electricity, no drains, no mains water and no road. To get there meant a trek across two fields with only the wheel tracks of a horse-drawn waggon to guide you between the gorse bushes, blackthorn and brambles. Emmett butts (ant hills) abounded and in the spring it displayed a mass of orchids. The advantages were self-evident when one made the effort to get there; the view across Marsh Vale was worth a fortune. The solitude was broken by continual bird song from dawn to dusk and then the night shift took over for there were nightingales, foxes, badgers, bats and owls. The water supply was the best tasting anywhere, coming straight out of the hill directly behind the house, and who worried about drains? Everything just ran away down the hill and disappeared. The only person they ever saw was the postman and he came on foot, pushing his bicycle across the fields from Hewingbere or Cowcroft Farms. He was an excuse for a cup of tea and of course, as well as letters he was the bringer of all the news that had occurred since his last visit. He would take letters to post or deliver anything to North Perrott which was his last port of call.

They were pretty well self-sufficient for they did a bit of gardening and the shotgun ensured a regular supply of meat. There were deer in abundance, pheasant, partridge, duck and hare, according to season. Pigeon and rook for pies, rabbits for stewing at any time of year and for a special treat in the winter, badger; Badger feasts were an annual event held in most pubs in the area. This was an occasion to meet friends and sample the farmhouse cider pressed from the apples grown in the orchard below the house. The fire was fuelled by fallen timber collected from the wood behind the house and illumination was by oil lamp and candles. On a winter evening the room could be very snug with the heat from the black range and the Aladdin paraffin lamp on the kitchen table which they sat around and rolled scraps of newspaper into spills for lighting the range and the pipe. Once made, these were then stored in an old jam jar on the mantelpiece.

Flossie or "Aunt Floss" as she was known locally, was a huge woman who took eggs that her hens had laid up to North Perrott for her special customers; the eggs were brown and speckled and were presented in a wicker basket lined with sweet-smelling hay that was probably more weeds than grass which accounted for the heady perfume of it. No one could resist them. Her husband Ernie on the other hand was a slight man, very wiry and weather-beaten who farmed the few acres that they had and relied on local farmers to help him out when things got a bit hectic around hay making season. They didn't mind, because Aunt Floss always provided a feast at lunch and at supper time and there was the never-ending supply of cider made from Ernie's Kingstone Black cider apples.

One very hot and sunny day in late June they were turning a field of hay by hand; Father had mown it a couple of days before and they were turning the swathes of mown grass over to let the sun dry the underneath before they could sweep it into a hayrick.

Ernie wouldn't hire Father to do anything by machine that he could do or get done by hand in exchange for a gallon or two of cider.

They heard the air-raid siren sometime after noon but took no notice; they didn't hear any aircraft and the all-clear went soon afterwards so nothing interrupted the steady swish of their picks and wooden rakes as they worked their way around the field. Ernie stopped, straightened up and took a watch out of his waistcoat pocket.

"Once more round Floss, and we'll stop for a spot of dinner. I'd bedder get another jar o' cider." He stuck the prongs of his pick in the ground and strolled up across the field to replenish the vital liquid, while Flossie worked her way to the end of the row she was on and then followed him up over the hill. Ernie had judged things quite well because by the time he returned with the cider the rest of the gang were now close to the gate.

"Wet yer whistles a minute, lads. Floss says I've got to go back for the stew, 'tis too heavy for her ta carry." He returned shortly afterwards carrying a large iron pot that held about five gallons of rabbit stew that had been simmering away since dawn, followed closely by Floss carrying a large basket holding dishes, plates, spoons and loaves of bread. He put the pot on the ground removing the piece of sacking wrapped around the handle to protect his hands from the heat. He removed the lid and bent forward to inspect the contents; as he did so a shower of hayseeds that had taken up temporary residence on the brim of his hat fell into the open vessel.

"You stupid girt Mommet (scarecrow)! What be'ee doing?" exclaimed Flossie frantically, trying to scoop them out before they sank without trace. Not that there was much likelihood of that, the stew being too thick. She was interrupted by someone saying,

"Hark! What's that?" They all listened and could hear an aircraft, but it didn't sound quite as it should. Then they spotted it, moving south, not very quickly, with smoke coming from its starboard engine. They watched in silence for a while trying to make out what make it was.

"Is it one of ours?" someone asked.

"Shouldn't think so," came the reply. "If 'twere one of ours he'd be heading for Westlands or Yeovilton I should think." The question was quickly answered when they spotted the cross on the wings. Then a small black dot detached itself from the plane and turned into a parachute.

"He've baled out!" Someone stated the obvious.

"Ern, get your gun. If 'e's a Jerry, shoot the bugger!" The excitement mounted.

"Look, 'e's coming this way. What shall us do?" I couldn't say who had said what; it was a chorus, with everyone talking at once. By now, he was only about five hundred feet up and coming right for the middle of Ern's hay-field. Everyone ran towards him with pitchforks and rakes at the ready and he dropped into a ring of steel and wooden spikes. He was hardly an airman; he was not much more than a boy, and a terrified one at that. He stood to attention with his arms straight up in the air. He found this difficult as he was still attached to his parachute which in the gentle breeze was tugging at his shoulders. One of the ancient Britons came to his rescue and speared the parachute with his pitchfork and pinned it to the ground, while someone else pointed to the buckle to indicate that he should undo it, which he did, shooting his arms straight back up into the air immediately afterwards.

What to do with him? He obviously spoke no English and the locals around Moultons had little occasion to make use of German; the only words they knew were Adolf Hitler, Messerschmitt, and Opel. The only reason they knew that Opel was a German word was that the Rector had an Opel car; nasty, noisy thing.

A hurried council of war ensued until Floss put the priorities in front of them.

"Look, boys. Yer dinner's getting cold and we've got a field of hay to finish turning; the sun won't bide out all night." Words of wisdom indeed. Everyone sat down, including the German Luftwaffe, who was given the lid of the stew pot, a spoon, a slice of bread and two ladles of rabbit stew. He looked a little happier when he found that he wasn't going to be murdered. At least, he didn't think he was because it would have been a waste of some most excellent stew. He kept showing his appreciation by pointing at his helping and smiling while making appreciative noises that sounded like "Danke." Floss gave him another ladleful and some more bread saying,

"Of course 'ee can dunk it if 'ee wants to m'dear." Then someone else, realising that he was probably thirsty like the rest of them, handed him the cider jar.

By the time he had consumed all that stew and about a quart of cider he couldn't have run away, even if he had wanted to. While the refreshment break had been in progress a decision had been arrived at. He should, by rights, be taken to Crewkerne police station, but they would need two men to guard him and one to drive, they couldn't do it in under an hour and a half, perhaps two if there were forms to fill out and they couldn't spare either the time or the manpower. They would finish the hay first!

They got him to take off his jacket and they gave him a rake. Fortunately someone had brought two pitchforks, saying that was so he could change over when one got too hot, but they wouldn't trust the German with anything sharp. They pointed at someone using a rake, pointed at the German and then pointed at the hay. He got the message. The stew had made him sweat and he quenched his thirst frequently from the cider jar to which he seemed to have unrestricted access and he sang as he raked the hay. Ern couldn't believe his luck, having an extra hand to help out, this chap was no trouble, he worked well, almost frantically and he didn't ask damn fool questions or indulge in idle chit chat.

They finished the field just as it was getting dusk and Flossie had put on a spread of fresh-baked bread with cheese that would take the roof of your mouth off and onions pickled in cider and mint; of course, washed down with more cider. It was dark by the time they had finished supper and it was time to take their prisoner into Crewkerne. The menfolk decided it was necessary for all of them to go to be on the safe side, leaving Floss to do the washing up. Their prisoner was no trouble; the moment he lay down in the back of the waggon, he fell asleep. They had to go through Haselbury Plucknett to get to Crewkerne and going up Swan Hill they couldn't resist the temptation to call in at the Swan and show off their prize. The pub emptied out into the road and they all had a look at the German, who didn't wake up. Then off they set again to tackle the mile long Crewkerne Hill. They eventually arrived at Crewkerne police station and handed over their prize to a very surprised copper who seemed to know more about horses and waggons proceeding along the King's highway in the dark without lights, than he did about German prisoners of war. Anyway, he suggested that they had better not go back by the main road whence they had come as cars had masks on their headlights to stop the beam from shining up into the sky, and it would be difficult for motorists to spot an unlit waggon full of inebriated farmers. So they went home via Misterton and North Perrott, stopping briefly at the Globe and White Swan in Misterton and the Manor Arms in North Perrott to tell their tale. Closing time didn't come into it; if the pub looked closed they just stopped outside and shouted until someone emerged. No one knows what time they got home, because Floss had gone to bed and they didn't remember the next day.

It appeared that the plane struggled on and reached the channel before it came down and they heard later that troops and police had been mobilised to look for the pilot because someone up in Hardington had seen the parachute but lost sight of it when it disappeared behind a hill. They think he had been involved in a raid on Bristol docks and the rest of the crew had baled out when they were first hit. The pilot obviously thought he could make it back to friendly soil but didn't quite manage it. Even if he had done, I don't think he would have had a better welcome than Aunt Flossie's rabbit stew, cheese and pickled onions and Ernie's cider; on reflection, Ern thought that was the best field of hay he ever made.

Harvesting

I used to enjoy harvesting best of all, the sound of the binder and the gorgeous smell of the corn and the fragrant weeds that were crushed by the tractor wheels; and of course there were the rabbits! I used to walk behind the binder with a stick and usually the cutter bar was set high enough to clear the weeds, and the rabbits that used to "freeze" while the binder went over them were sometimes a little slow to react when daylight reappeared and a quick knock on the head ensured rabbit stew for dinner again. As the binder started cutting from the outside edge of the field, the rabbits, usually plenty in those days would move further into the corn to what they thought was safety. Usually the farmer and several friends would ring the remaining corn and blast away with their shotguns as the rabbits, realising that their hiding place was becoming non-existent would make a dash for the hedge. As a rule, the gunners were well disciplined and wouldn't fire until the rabbits were outside the circle of guns, but on one occasion

I remember, Eric Gatcombe, who was one of our tractor drivers, was unfortunately in the line of fire and was peppered with No. 5 shot from a 12 bore and had to be taken to hospital where one of the doctors remarked that the resulting X Ray picture looked like a photograph of frog spawn.

The Oxenburys at White Vine Farm were reaping one day. I'm not sure who was driving, either Dave or Phil, but it was a hot day and the one who was riding the binder (someone had to, to adjust the setting of the fans or the height of the cutter bar and make sure the knotter was working and hadn't run out of twine), well, he went to sleep and shortly afterwards the one driving the tractor did the same and when they woke up, they found themselves in the middle of the cornfield. On another occasion, Marion, Phil's wife was driving the tractor with a side rake on the back turning two rows of hay into one ready for the baler and didn't realise that the side rake had become unhitched until she drove into it on the next time around the field.

Marion, neé Budden of Kingswood Farm, next to Whitevine, had a brother Leon who drove an old but large Morris car. The mere fact that their farm was reached from Common Lane by a long, rough and very muddy track way before they made a concrete short cut was enough to cause the vehicle some distress which gave it a most unroadworthy appearance resulting him being stopped by the police in Yeovil curious to know whether he had any brakes. You know the drill.

"Good morning sir, Are you the owner of this vehicle?" Leon admitted that he was.

"Do you mind if we give you a little brake test?" Leon said that he didn't, whilst inwardly quaking in his boots. He used to do his own servicing, but only when his car became completely undriveable, which it almost was at that time.

"If you will drive at thirty miles an hour, we will follow you and when we blow our horn you put your brakes on." Strangely, they spoke in English and didn't ask him to proceed or apply his brakes as one would have expected; so off they set. Thirty miles an hour was reached, and almost immediately, "BEEP". Leon put both feet down hard, to be on the safe side he grabbed the handbrake and pulled with all his considerable strength with his left hand and on the steering wheel with his right. The car shuddered to a halt and Leon waited, sweating. A face with a cap appeared in his open window.

"That seems to be satisfactory, Sir," said the policeman looking somewhat concerned seeing Leon holding a detached quarter of the rim of his steering wheel in his right hand while the remains of it resembled the control column of a Lancaster bomber.

"It would seem, Sir, that you might need a new one of those. Good morning, drive carefully."

Another delight was walking in the furrow behind the plough and smelling the freshly turned earth. Tractor drivers these days, with their heated, air-conditioned stereo cabs miss all these treats; all the tractor driver had in the '40s was a West of England sack over his shoulders held in place with a 3" nail.

Of course, since 1940 we had double summer time which meant it was still daylight at about 11 o' clock at night and it seemed inexcusable that I was put to bed at about seven and had to try to sleep through Father banging about under my bedroom window for about four hours.

When one has agricultural machinery to operate, there is the inevitable occasional breakage so Father went off to Southampton University to take a course on oxy-acetylene welding. He stayed with his sister Elsie Sims who lived in Southampton; all his brothers and sisters moved away from Hardington: Tom to Romsey, Emmie to North Baddesley, Minnie to the Isle of White, Jack to Chelmsford, George to Shoeburyness and Frank to London. Father's birthday was on 11th January and the whole family held a reunion at Frank's every year. Doodlebugs didn't stop a Rendell reunion. I remember the bombed buildings and the windows that were intact being treated to a St Andrew's cross of brown parcel tape to reduce the shards of flying glass caused by blast from a nearby bomb. Frank's house was on the corner of Leigham Vale and Palace Road and right opposite was an iron railway bridge that electric trains ran over day and night. The noise they made was extremely loud but you can sleep through anything once you get used to it.

Once, I actually went to London on my own, aged about seven. I had been by train on several occasions and was confident that I knew the route. Father put me on the train at Yeovil Junction and off I went. It was so simple; the train didn't go further than Waterloo, that was the end of the line. Then I just walked out of the station to catch a number 68 or 68a bus to West Norwood which went through Brixton, past the Kennington Oval cricket ground, Herne Hill cycle track and Stockwell Park. Then I got off just before the railway bridge and walked, dragging my suit case up Leigham Vale to number 70, later re-numbered 100, when they built some extra houses. It seemed a long way, but I eventually arrived at Aunt Jessie's and rang the doorbell.

"Hello dear," she said. "Where's father?" She took a bit of persuading that I was alone. I think it was on that occasion when I was treated to the experience of a British Restaurant meal. I seem to remember it was mainly potatoes with some gravy for which we queued for some time and sat down at a long table with a lot of other people in a large room; I don't know what its original use was. We had walked down Leigham Vale to the bottom of the road and turned right under the railway bridge where I liked to watch the sparks from the overhead tram wires as they roared through; then we walked about half way up the hill in West Norwood along a very wide pavement to find our destination on the right.

Anyway, when Father came back from his welding course he wanted to practise on something, so he made me a steel scabbard for my wooden dagger, with of course a loop to thread my belt through. That's something I remember, my trousers only had three loops for the belt then, two at the front and one at the back, to save material I suppose. Now I have six!

Father utilised his new welding skill in constructing a trailer to go behind the tractor. He obtained several lengths of 4" x 2" steel channel from F.W. Sibley's in Goldcroft, Yeovil and started welding them together. At that time I had a brown Cocker Spaniel that strayed in one day as a pup and I called him Bobby. He liked company and would often go into the garage to watch people doing things. In the side door of the garage, Father, or more likely Grandfather, had cut a cat hole and to comply with the blackout regulations at the time, Father had nailed a sack bag over the hole, like a curtain, to prevent light from spilling out. Well, Bobby often used to sit behind the curtain with his head in the hole looking out and whimpering for someone to open the door because the hole was too small for him to get through. Father was welding away with a number thirty five or forty five nozzle on his torch, anyway it was a big one and had a good pool of molten steel joining two pieces of channel together when he had a blow-back; a most enormous BANG, coinciding with a shower of sparks and molten metal flying across the garage floor. There was a thump at the far end of the garage and when Father looked, there was no sign of Bobby, he'd gone out through the cat hole!

I must have seen lots of films in those days but only one comes vividly to mind, apart from the Disney ones, and that was *One of our Aircraft is Missing* in 1942. Then there were the newsreels with the commentary read so concisely and dramatically in Oxford English and the cartoon, sometimes "Popeye the Sailor" or Mickey Mouse and Donald Duck with Goofy in attendance. We had three cinemas in Yeovil then. The Gaumont, was on the corner of South Street and Stars Lane. If you go up South Street and look back at the brick wall of the building, you can still just see the black camouflage paint that was used to disguise the premises. By the way, whoever was responsible for the project to camouflage Yeovil and the Westland Aircraft factory must have done a remarkably efficient job, because even the local pilots could only find the airfield by using the two water towers as reference points. There used to be one at the end of Elliot's Drive and one at High Lea. The Odeon was at the junction of Court Ash and Kingston with a grand entrance sporting copper handrails to assist patrons up and down the entrance steps. The third was the Central Cinema, a small privately owned theatre in Church Street which is now the entrance to the solicitor's complex. I remember the two big cinemas with their Wilton carpet and worsted velvet upholstery which smelled of opulence and cigar smoke, while now the present multiplex cinema stinks of popcorn. I must admit I seldom frequent the establishment these days.

The other sign of the times were the "pill boxes", concrete structures like little hexagonal huts with little square windows; they were placed at strategic places like cross roads where they might have a clear view of any approaching enemy and be in a position to protect the defending troops from enemy fire. Some were disguised as hay ricks being covered in hay and thatched. The one at the top of Hendford Hill has only recently been demolished and the one at Houndstone Corner was preserved by constructing a building over it when the new housing estate was built. It's on

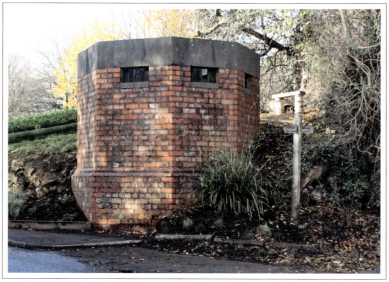

World War Two pill box.

the corner of Bluebell Road and Wisteria Close, Brympton. They are listed monuments now.

The West Coker parishioners dug themselves a cave at the bottom of Chur Lane, being on the strata of Yeovil Sands, a layer of hardish sandstone from which Hamstone is quarried at the end of the escarpment at Hamdon Hill. Odcombe, too had caves, two of them, but there is some discussion as to whether they were dug as air raid shelters or for potato storage. There is also one at the bottom of Chinnock Hollow. Odcombe had, on the Chinnock road, an underground bunker to house the men who lit decoy fires during an air raid. There were 40 gallon oil drums situated in the fields with inflammable contents that were ignited at the warning of an impending raid to fool the bomber crews into thinking that someone had already dropped bombs on Westlands and that the fires were the target. Not much fun for the Odcombe residents, but I expect most of them were working at Westland's anyway.

There was an anti-aircraft gun emplacement in Emmet Butt ground on Haselbury Park Farm near to the gateway in Common Lane, that leads to Kingswood and Whitevine Farms. One afternoon Father took me down to the New Road between Hardington Marsh and Haselbury to see a number of biplanes lined up under the hedge of Seven Acres, one of Farmer Foot's fields, and we watched as they were started in turn and took off. On another occasion, we went to look at a Fairey Swordfish that had made a forced landing in the field at the top of Barrows Hill and unable to stop in time, finished up in the road near the top of Chant's Lane.

One of the strangest coincidences of the war was the handing in, to Father, of a door off an aeroplane that had been found between Pendomer and Hardington Marsh. On relating this to Uncle Frank, whose son Alan was a pilot, he said, "Alan lost the door of his Beaufighter over the west country somewhere." We never found out for certain that it was off a Beaufighter because it was just handed in to the police station and they probably passed it on to Yeovilton.

Alan had a sister, Diana, who during the war was in the auxiliary fire service, and during one of our family reunions in London she came off duty and hung up her tin hat on the hook on the back of the kitchen door.

"We had a strange one today," she said. "We had to go to a house that had been bombed where someone was trapped under the rubble. When we dug this old chap out wearing just his pyjama top he was laughing. 'What do you find so funny?' I asked him.

"I just went to the toilet and pulled the chain and the whole bloody house fell down."

On a subsequent visit to Frank and Jessie in London, we were introduced to a new "Dining Table"; it was about 6' long and 4' wide and 30" high made out of steel. It was a Morrison shelter, with legs constructed out of 6" x 6" angle with rails top and bottom out of

Tank trap.

3" x 2" angle with a sheet steel top 1/8" thick and sides made out of 3" x 2" steel square mesh. The idea was that it would support the weight of fallen masonry and give one a safe cell while one waited to be dug out. They were supplied to people living in houses without a cellar and if the combined income of the household was less than £400 it was free. I remember going around London by the "Underground" and seeing all the bunk beds on the platforms where people spent the night during air raids and there were plenty of them.

Another piece of architecture that sprang up was the blast wall. We had a large east window at Hardington school, and we returned from one holiday to find that a huge brick wall had been built in front of it to shield it from the blast of an explosion that would have sent showers of glass fragments into the classroom. They also built one across the front door, leaving just enough room to squeeze around the ends to get in. Then there were the static water tanks, many in and around Yeovil. They were usually square brick compounds, about 5 feet high, that were kept full mainly by rainwater collected off the roofs of adjacent buildings. Each held hundreds of gallons of water and was there as an emergency supply for the fire brigade should the water mains become ruptured. Strangely, they seemed to be a magnet to old bicycles and prams

Then there were the tank traps. Concrete cubes with pyramidal tops to be placed across the road in the event of an invasion. I would have thought the tanks could have gone through the hedge into the field and avoided them.

After the war, going up Warden Hill at Evershot on the A37, on the left-hand side there was a field full of these concrete blocks and they stayed there for years. Further on along Long Ash Lane, near the turning to Cattistock, was a large oak tree by the side of the road that had a sentry box built in its branches. That stayed there for an extremely long time until it gradually fell to bits. The tree was eventually felled in a road improvement scheme to make the junction safer.

What did I do in the evenings, I'm sometimes asked. In the summer with the lighter nights I spent hours out in the fields with my spaniel Bobby or damming the stream to make it deep enough to float a boat. My best friend Brian and I used to make bows and arrows from the abundant materials around and see if we could get the arrows to go high enough to clear the telephone wires.

In the winter Father and I used to make up bicycle wheels. Fitting the spokes in the correct order and pattern was not as easy as it might first appear, and the more people that got involved with suggestions, the worse it was. Then, once put together correctly it had to be "trued" to make it run smoothly without wobbling sideways or hopping up and down. This was achieved by tightening or slackening off the nut or "nipple" at the end of the spokes. Another thing Father taught me on dark winter evenings was to tie knots; it has stood me in good stead ever since. His favourites were the "Clove Hitch" and the "Sheet Bend" which for some reason he preferred to the "Reef Knot". Another winter activity or event was the "Badger Feast" held at the New Inn, renamed the Mandeville Arms in the 1960s. Apparently, only the hams were cooked and it was noted that they made one hell of a mess of your oven as they were very fatty and splattered everywhere.

Visitors

In 1943 we had a visitor in the shape of Gervaise Rendell who was in the 48th Canadian Highlanders. He was one of our relations from Nova Scotia on his way to fight in Sicily. He was wounded in Sicily and put on a hospital ship heading for Great Britain. He unfortunately died from gangrene poisoning and was buried at sea. Later his body was washed up on the shores of Tripoli where he was eventually laid to rest.

Another visitor we had, in the guise of an evacuee was Uncle Jack's parrot, "Rosie" from Chelmsford. She was put in her cage on a table by the side of the fireplace. I tried hard to make her talk, but I think cockatoos make better talkers than grey and pink Galahs. Anyway, Rosie chucked her seeds here and there, as parrots do, and made a right old mess. Mother decided to clear this up, so to make it easier to pull out the table to sweep behind, she put Rosie on the window sill. Rosie had been clinging onto the bars of her cage with her beak during the transporting operation and when she came to rest. she let go, marched sideways to the middle of her perch, fluffed up her feathers and said, "Coo, innit cold." Those were the only words that parrot ever spoke. We used to let her out in the evenings and she had a favourite perch which was on the head of one of the two black buck heads that were mounted on the wall of the living room. They

Rosie.

were shot by Uncle Tom on one of his postings in the army. She would sit between the horns and meditate. Then one evening came a knock at the door and who should be there but Tommy Voisey of Marsh Farm. He was one of the Churchwardens and had come to discuss some church business. He sat on one of the high ladderback chairs and hung his bowler hat, which he had politely removed, on the back of an adjacent chair. He hadn't noticed Rosie and we had forgotten she was out when Tommy started on his speech. Rosie seemed to show an interest in the sermon and made her way quietly from the head of the buck to the top of the curtains. I was sitting right opposite and saw her progress along the curtain until she was right above Tommy, then she abseiled, beak and claws, down the curtain and perched on the chair supporting Tommy's bowler hat. She looked at it with first one eye and then the other and then picked it up with her beak. I wondered what she would do next. Not long to wait; she stood on one leg, gripped the rim of the hat with the free claw and, "chomp", just like a ticket inspector. She spat out the morsel of brim and moved it round an inch. "Chomp," again a piece of brim dropped to the floor, and she continued until she had reached the point from which she had started, where she thought, "done that" and promptly dropped the titfer, now resembling a gear wheel, to the floor. Tommy, still talking, heard it go down and reached for it and picked it up. Father, who had also been watching with bitten lip and raised eyebrow said nothing. He wasn't that keen on Tommy anyway. Tommy never got to the end of his speech and while he was surveying the damage to his hat, Rosie had taken the opportunity to return, as she had come, to the safety of the buck's head. Tommy inspected his hat in great detail, bending the little bits of brim this way and that. Then he tried it on; I'm not sure whether it was to see if it still fitted, or whether it was his. Tommy left, hat in hand, certain that we had rats. It cost Father a new bowler, but he said it was worth it. I used to see his new hat frequently, because when he came to church on Sunday mornings, he drove up from the Marsh in a pony and trap and tied the pony up outside the back gate to the Rectory at the bottom of Rectory Lane then walked up to the church.

Also at that time I had a pet pigeon. Grandfather had made a dovecote which sat on a tall pole at the corner of the lawn. Originally, the cote held several fan tail and tumbler pigeons which over the years must have died off for it stood empty. Then one day a visitor dropped in, probably a homing pigeon that didn't want to go home, and he came indoors. On being given some crumbs, he decided to take up residence in the vacant property across the lawn. He seemed to like company, because he would come in through the fanlight and spend hours with me and his favourite game was hide and seek amongst the cushions on the settee. He only misbehaved once, when I startled him. He used to follow Mother to school every day, much to the amusement of the children, because he would come in through the open window and perch on the top of the blackboard until it was time to go home; then he would fly from tree to tree keeping pace with her until they were both safely home again. One night we had a dreadful storm and we never saw him again. We never knew what happened to him and missed him dreadfully as did the children at the school.

Fred Fudge

Another occasion involving Tommy Voisey was with one Fred Fudge. Fred lived with his sister on Coker Hill. He was a little man, slightly portly with a noticeable limp and elderly bicycle.

He was dressed, as suited his profession, with leather boots, heavily hob-nailed, and brown corduroy trousers caught up just below the knee with brown leather straps called "Yorks". Yorks served several purposes, the first to keep the trouser bottoms above ankle height and therefore out of the mud. Secondly, to keep them baggy about the knees so that it wasn't necessary to hitch them up every time he knelt or bent down. Thirdly it prevented cold draughts, or worse still a mouse from invading his nether regions; an occupational hazard during some seasons of the year. Fourthly they prevented the trousers from becoming trapped in the bicycle chain wheel.

His shirt was long and heavy, being made of white flannel with a red stripe running through it. It was collarless with an ivory and gold stud threaded through one of the top buttonholes. This was covered with a grey herringbone tweed waistcoat with most of the buttons missing. One of the button-holes supported a silver plated watch chain which was now mostly copper, the silver plate having been worn off long since by continually checking the time on a huge turnip watch concealed in the left hand pocket. The other end of the chain was attached to a silver bladed fruit knife used for peeling apples and kept in the right hand pocket. Over all was a Harris Tweed jacket whose pockets had almost pulled themselves away from the coat to expose the corner of a well-used tobacco tin and a large red and white handkerchief. The huge handkerchief could be used for carrying bread and cheese, mopping the brow, tying around the neck to keep out hayseeds, over the nose and mouth to keep out dust, over the eyes if one was working in a saw pit, or as a triangular bandage in case of accident. A most versatile piece of equipment. The ensemble was finished off with a wide-brimmed battered brown felt hat, which through years of rain, sweat, dust and smoke, had moulded itself to the shape of his head, like a type of fungus surmounting a tree stump.

His bicycle was rather special. Because of his aforementioned limp it did service mostly as a walking frame. Occasionally on the flat and downhill it was ridden and always it had Fred's tool of his trade tied to the crossbar with binder twine.

This tool was a four pronged pick or dung fork, known in the vernacular as a "Dung Verk". It had a handle about 5 feet long and the tines were wickedly sharp through constant use and glinted in the sunlight. When lashed to the crossbar with the teeth facing forward it made the bicycle a potentially lethal weapon if ever the brakes failed. (Boadicea would have been proud.) The reason the prongs faced forward and not to the rear will be made clear. It was all to do with Fred's "hoppy" leg which made it very difficult to mount a bicycle in the normal fashion. Thus his machine had been modified to accommodate the disability. The left-hand nut on the rear wheel spindle had been replaced by a piece of threaded tube four inches long to make a foot rest. Remember this was fifty years before the B.M.X. bike was produced! Half way up the rear fork, again on the left hand side was clamped another step, so let's climb aboard.

Stand on the left of the bicycle holding the handlebars. Stand on left foot with right foot on extended nut and push off with left foot in scooter mode. Now with cycle rolling, lift left foot up to step on rear forks, transfer weight to left foot and swing right leg around rear mudguard and lower nether regions onto saddle, locate feet onto pedals and if still in forward motion commence pedalling. All this took as long to execute as it does to describe and often forward motion and subsequent balance had been lost before getting under way with the resulting requirement of having to go back to position one. This of course is after extricating ones personage from amongst or beneath bicycle and tool of trade and occasionally from clump of nettles or roadside ditch if one had been particularly unfortunate. As this happened frequently if Fred was attempting to execute the mounting procedure on level, or slightly rising ground, one is sympathetic to the fact that Fred wanted his fork as far away as possible from his exercises at the rear of his bicycle. Fortunately, traffic in Hardington then was scarce and not a problem, thus Fred had plenty of time and space for his manoeuvres.

Now, as you have no doubt gathered, Fred was a professional muck spreader. There was a different system in those days; tractors were coming in but there were still plenty of horses about and cowstalls were cleaned out twice a day after milking and the muck in the yard and stalls was mixed with straw and stacked to rot down. If the heap was turned and the bacteria left to work, most of the offensive smell disappeared leaving one with a dry substance of a peaty nature. This was loaded onto a horse drawn two-wheeled tipping cart called a "Putt" and taken out into the fields to be dropped in heaps of about half a ton, some eight to ten yards apart, depending on how intensively it was needed. There it was left for Fred to get to work on it with his fork to fling it here and there and spread it evenly on the ground.

Well, one day he was engaged in his occupation down in Big Johnathan, a field down in Hardington Marsh on the north side of the New Road leading from Hardington Marsh to Haselbury Plucknett, when Tommy Voisey was coming home from Crewkerne in his pony and trap. Tommy sees Fred working in the field and reins in at the gateway.

"Yer, Fred."

"Yes, Maister?"

"Come yer a minnit."

The pony, realising that a long conversation was imminent, decided that he had time for a spot of lunch so lunged towards a particularly succulent batch of weeds in the hedgerow that he had spotted on his way to Crewkerne.

"Whoa," said Tommy. "Bide still will'ee?" and he took off his bowler hat to mop his brow with a spotted handkerchief while he waited for Fred, who was coming, but not very fast because of his limp.

"A bit hot for your job innit Fred?" he said as Fred reached the five-bar gate and draped himself over it.

"Ah, 'tiz. The way the vlies be bitin' I reckon we be goin' t' 'ave some thunder. Wass thee want I vor anyroad?"

"I've got a cow died up on Dancing Hill, could you bury en vor I?"

Nowadays one picks up the phone and a man comes with a four wheel drive pick-up with a winch and its all tidy in half an hour. No such luxuries then.

"Reckon zoo," said Fred.

"Termorrer do?" Fred asked.

"Saddernoon ood be bedder, 'coz 'er's already beginning to blow up. Anyway, do the best you can. I'll let 'ee finish what you be doin'" and he drove off with the pony doing his best not to drop the portion of greenery he was at that moment trying to dispose of.

That afternoon, after a hunk of bread and cheese and a bottle of cold tea, Fred made his way to Dancing Hill; a high point on the county boundary between Hardington Mandeville, Somerset and Halstock, Dorset. He picked his way through brambles, blackthorn bushes, gorse and "Emmet Butts" (ant hills) until he found the cow. So then he set to work. If he dug a hole directly behind the cow, he could just roll it in. Farmer was right, the carcase was indeed beginning to inflate due to the gasses produced from the vegetation in the cow's stomachs. The trouble was, Fred's tool was a fork and although he made a fair enough job of digging the turf away, it did no more than break up the subsoil after that. He needed a spade, so he set off down to the farm to borrow one. The best part of a mile each way and the sun was beginning to burn him up like a jacket potato in all his heavy clothes which he never seemed to consider removing. He filled up his empty tea bottle with water from the dairy while he had the chance, procured a spade and returned to his contract. He looked at the cow; he was sure it was now bigger than when he left it and the left legs were no longer resting on the ground. Anyway, he made better progress with the spade and dug away until nearly sunset. He had nearly two and a half miles to go home after he had reached the road and it was nearly all uphill. Also, his sister worried if he was out after dark so he left the spade and his fork resting against the cow and made tracks.

When Fred came back after breakfast the next morning, the sun had already been up since four smiling down on his project and when he saw the cow he nearly dropped his bottle of cold tea; it resembled a huge hairy piggy bank lying on its side and much too fat to fit into the existing hole that he had been digging the day before, so the first job was to widen the existing hole before he went any deeper. So he set to work with a new sense of urgency.

By ten thirty he had widened the hole sufficiently and stopped for a swig of warm tea. His trousers were sticking to his legs and his hat was several shades of brown darker where it was wet through with his perspiration. He had hoped that by dinner time he would have dug the hole deep enough, so back to work he went again. The sun was merciless and the carcase was beginning to smell dreadfully, with no breeze to carry the scent away; and down in the hole it was hotter than ever. Every time he stopped to straighten his back, he dragged his tweed covered forearm across his brow and neck to wipe away the sweat. Was it his imagination, or was the cow getting bigger than ever? It now resembled a blown-up rubber glove. Panic set in. He was certain that it was growing faster than he was digging the hole. As soon as he had dug the hole big enough, it was bigger than the hole again. It never dawned on him to stick his fork into the side of the cow to let the gas out. He dug frantically, afraid that the cow would burst and bury him in rotting entrails. By three o' clock he had decided that it was now or never and he tried to roll the cow into the hole. He lifted the back leg but the middle and the front of the cow refused to move. Next he tried lifting the front leg with no success. Then he grabbed the tail and tried to pull in the direction of the hole. The only result this had was to release an enormous gush of evil-smelling gas from the cow's rear end which forced him to leave the immediate area until he could catch his breath again. While he was gasping for air, he noticed a rail in the hedge, stopping a gap; so he fetched it and started levering under the cow's middle. Eventually he was successful and with much gasping and straining from Fred the cow rolled into the hole. "Thud," flat on its back with its four legs straight up in the air…and Fred hadn't dug the hole deep enough!. The hole was deep enough for the body, but the legs were sticking up above ground level like four traffic bollards; he hadn't considered the legs in his calculation as he was only concentrating on the size of the body. He hopped from one rigid limb to the other, trying to bend them down below ground level but rigormortis had long since set in and they were firm enough to hang a gate on. So he resigned himself to covering over the body and at about tea time he patted down the earthy mound between the four sentinels, tied the fork and spade to his crossbar and wearily wended his way down off the hill between the gorse, brambles, blackthorn and Emmet Butts to draw his wages.

"Finished then, Fred?" enquired Tommy, when Fred lurched into the yard.

"Reckon zo," said Fred in a non-committal sort of fashion, holding out the hand that didn't have the bicycle in it.

"Be you goin' to leave the spade, or shall I knock a bit off what I do owe 'ee?"

Fred released the spade from his crossbar in silence, handed it back to Tommy, took his wages and went wearily home for his tea, absolutely shattered and a nervous wreck.

For the next few weeks he made sure he was not working anywhere he would be likely to run into or be seen by Tommy, but his luck ran out eventually. He was coming up Bridgeclose Hill from Hardington Marsh to Hill End late one Saturday morning. It was his half-day and he wanted to call at Bert Rendell's for a new twin-cell battery for the front light of his bicycle on his way home for his dinner.

He could hear Tommy's pony and trap coming along Marsh Road and he prayed that Tommy was going to Crewkerne, but his heart sank when he heard it turn and head up Bridgeclose Hill. He was no match for Tommy's pony going downhill, let alone up so he resigned himself to an undesired confrontation. In no time at all the pony was alongside and the pony, used to Tommy having conversations with people he met on the road, slowed to the same velocity as Fred in anticipation for some sort of discourse. He even twiddled his ears round to take the best advantage of the ensuing dialogue.

"I've been keeping my eye out for you, Fred.

"'ave 'ee maister? 'ows that then?"

" I thought I asked'ee to bury that cow up on Dancing Hill?"

"Zo I did, Maister."

"No you didn', his legs be stickin' up out o' ground."

"Ah, tha's they bloody foxes bin up there diggin' o'n up."

"Don' talk so daft Fred, what be I goin' to do wi' en?"

"I should leave'em until about hay making time Maister, the mowing machine will hit 'em off."

By the time Fred got away from Tommy it was five past one when he arrived at Bert Rendell's and rang the bell.

A more unusual bell would be hard to find. It hung on a bracket outside the garage doors. It was a cylinder from a Radial aircraft engine complete with fins and the clapper was the con rod with a leather strap fitted to it and it made a noise that could be heard indoors or out, in the church, pub, or anywhere else in the village for that matter. So wherever Bert might happen to be, he could hear when he had a customer.

On this particular occasion Bert was in and went to see who was ringing the bell and there was Fred, all hot and bothered.

"Hello Fred. What can we do for you?"

"Baint you shut then?"

"No, we're not shut."

"Caw, an' I've come up from Marsh like bloody hell 'cos I was sure you'd be shut."

The thought of Fred going anywhere like bloody hell was beyond the imagination. Four miles an hour was the best he ever managed. He explained that he needed a new battery for his lamp and how Tommy Voisey had hindered him and then, because Father seemed to be sympathetic, poured out the story of the dead cow. I hope his sister wasn't keeping his dinner hot for him, for it must have been half past two by the time he reached home.

Pendomerites

Other people who came to church by pony and trap were the Pattens from Parsonage Farm, at Pendomer. I sometimes rode back with them after church on a Sunday morning to their farm just the other side of the railway line which came into view as you came through the arch of the railway bridge. The journey was a pleasant one, the pony trotting on seemingly effortlessly, with its ears pointing towards home, only occasionally twisting them round to catch a bit of conversation in case it was an instruction for him. I learned to balance the trap so there was not too much weight on the pony's back and not sitting at the back thereby lifting him off the ground. I would stay at the Patten's for lunch and Father would come for me at about four o' clock and after a cup of tea would take me home. The Pattens and my parents must have been

Parsonage Farm arch.

Wedding Parsonage Farm.

Wedding Group in Orchard. Back Row (L-R): No. 6 Back row, Bob Turner, Manor Farm, Hardington; No.s 8; 9; & 10, Aubrey White, Grove Farm, Hardington Marsh, Dulcie's brother, Frank & Dulcie Patten, then maybe Dulcie's parents, Theo and his wife. 2nd Row R – L, No.s 5 & 6, Probably Gladys and Winnie White, Dulcie's sisters Maybe Rev, Ransome, (Vicar of Pendomer) L behind Arthur. Vicar of Babcary R behind Margaret. Herbert (with dog) and Annie Patten, (bride's parents.) Extreme right with trilby hat and light suit, Roberta Rendell (my mother.) In front of my mother, small girl, bride's maid Annette Smith, with her father. Me, sitting on floor in front of the Groom.
On the left, standing next to the gent holding the small child is Jane Ransome, (my Nanny), from Hardington Moor.

Page boy.

quite friendly for I was a page boy at their daughter Margaret's wedding to Arthur Fry of East Chinnock. I remember my blue satin suit with the patent black shoes that were fastened with one small button to the bar that went across the instep. My companion, the bride's maid, was Annette Smith, who lived in Beer Street, Yeovil, not far from Crowther's engineering works. We both had almost matching hairstyles because I had a mass of tight curls at that time and remember being sick of ladies saying "Oh he ought to have been a girl." Strangely, I don't remember having seen her before nor since; but I do have a photograph of us both holding hands in the orchard at Pendomer.

P.O.W.s

Arthur Fry, on his farm at East Chinnock, as did others in the area, had German Prisoners of War working on his farm. They were housed at Houndstone Camp, between Montacute and Yeovil, wore dark blue boiler suits with a large yellow circular patch sewn on their backs. They were brought out each morning in army lorries and collected in the evening to be taken back to their secure accommodation. I became quite friendly with one in particular, but not at that time.

They used to amuse themselves when locked away by making things which they exchanged for cigarettes and Father acquired a ship in an orange squash bottle that one of them had made out of bits of scrap material. I still have it and treasure it. I remember seeing a toy that Arthur had in the shape of a table tennis bat with four chicken standing around the rim facing inwards with a length of thread from each to a single weight hanging underneath. If you rotated the bat in a horizontal circular movement, the chicken would bob up and down in a pecking manner which I thought most wonderful. As well as the chickens he had a cow that walked

Bottle.

down a slope. Its legs were like wheels let into the body fore and aft and were carved, or cut out, in a shape like the Isle of Man emblem, only there were four legs on each, not three. Placed on a draining board or any similar slope it would wobble its way to the bottom. Fascinating! Father also bought me a carved workman holding a saw vertically that had a weight on the end and if you stood him on the edge of the mantelpiece or the table and swung the weight he would industriously saw away like a sawyer cutting up boards at a saw pit. The third item I had was a model of a patrol boat, but because the keel had been made from a piece of lead it was too heavy to float, so sad to say I lost interest in it and I don't recall what was its outcome. I wish I had been aware at the time of its future memorabilia value in later years. The particular prisoner that Father bought these items from was one Gunther Anton; he was only sixteen years old and had been a tail gunner in the Luftwaffe. His aircraft was shot down over Bridgwater Bay and when he was captured, he was brought to Houndstone Camp.

These lads, as lads they were, being polite and industrious, were accepted into the life of East Chinnock and made lasting friendships with the natives, even unto death! Gunther, when he was repatriated, went home to Leonberg and told his father how well he had been treated by the British and felt that he would like to show his appreciation in some way. His father, who was a Glassmeister suggested that perhaps he might make a window for East Chinnock church; so he put the wheels in motion and contacted Rev. Percy Nicholls who was delighted to accept and secured the approval of the Diocese. So Gunther came over and took the necessary templates and went away to Germany to make up a stained glass window. He later returned and fitted it with great celebration which started a reciprocal visiting procedure lasting for many years. Today, contacts are still kept with those still alive.

Gunther then decided that perhaps he would make another, and then another, until he had re-glazed every window that was in plain glass and finished off by building a screen of glass bricks between the tower and the nave. I still have a pile of bricks that were left over! His final project in this country was to make two windows for my Father in Hardington church.

I went over to Neckarsulm with my Father on one of the exchange visits and we were right royally treated; they couldn't do enough for us, treating us to banquet after banquet.

We had left East Chinnock by coach at twenty past three one afternoon and didn't arrive in Neckarsulm until four o' clock the next afternoon after making a brief stop at Heidelberg. Our coach driver had nearly been shot by an armed policeman at the border at Aachen for leaving his engine idling; it was only for a minute while he waited for one of our party to come out of the toilet. At the party they had prepared in the Town Hall with all the local dignitaries,

East Chinnock.

I produced the ship in a bottle. They were in tears. I handed the bottle to Anton, warning him that he couldn't keep it, whereon he owned up to the fact that he didn't make it. One of the older prisoners was the craftsman and Gunther only got commission for selling them. Still who cares? We didn't realise it at the time, but we insulted our German hosts by leaving the party at about ten o' clock and it wasn't until several years later that I had the opportunity to put things right by explaining that our party were mostly elderly and they had been travelling for over twenty four hours on a coach and were absolutely shattered and couldn't keep awake. We visited the Audi factory and were fed, then went to the N.S.U. Museum and were fed again.

We had a tour of the vineyards and were given bottles of wine. We were invited to Rudi Benz winery where a huge party was arranged. In the tower at East Chinnock church there is a photograph of Gunther Anton with my accordion, John White and myself which was taken at Rudi's. It seems that every small village has an Oompah Band, for we went to Dahnfelt, a little village down the road, where we were fêted again to a huge meal in a rustic barn that had in the past been used for storing barrels of wine, while the band played enthusiastically accompanied by the locals, who thumped the tables in time to the music. The band later came over to Kiddlington near Oxford, where we went to hear them. On the Sunday, they informed us that their local priest, who spoke English, was on holiday and they had been trying hard to find a replacement so that they could perform the morning service entirely in English as a mark of respect, and praise the Lord they had been successful. He was from Pakistan! Well, he sounded English to them. What a memorable visit that was, they could not have done more to make us feel welcome. It certainly gave us a lot to talk about on the coach journey home.

Shopping, the Church and School

With Father working all hours and Mother not being able to drive, shopping was a bit of an exercise. The bus only came to Hardington on Mondays, Wednesdays and Fridays with two trips on Saturday; the late one supposedly to bring folks back from the pictures in Yeovil, but it left half an hour before the end of the last film which was pretty useless. There was a "Workman's Bus" at about six in the morning and again after work in the evening to collect and return all the people working in Westland's. Through natural wastage the number of passengers gradually decreased until only Percy Curtis was riding on it, which he did for what seemed years. Anyway, being at school Monday to Friday, left Mother with only Saturday to do any shopping or have her hair done in Perham's near the bottom of Middle Street; so she would catch the bus into Yeovil, then, after shopping, catch one back to West Coker then walk up Chur Lane and down over Hackings' Hill back to Hardington.

Ransome used to clean the church on Saturday mornings and took me with her. My job was to top up the oil lamps with paraffin; I remember I used to go home stinking of it. One thing Ransome did that I couldn't stand was to brush the coconut matting with a stiff brush. It set my teeth on edge and I used to keep out of earshot. At or about the time Mother's bus was due in at West Coker, I would climb up into the Vestry window (the organ wasn't back there then) watch for her to climb the stile at the top of Coker Ridge and then follow her progress down over the fields. The lane, that was the official route, was so full of trees and brambles as to make it impossible to navigate, so people created a footpath down over the fields adjacent to it. Down past the Black House where the Charles family lived and then she disappeared from view as she came down into North Lane, past Millcombe Pond and up the steep hill towards the church. Then I would go home with her while Ransome finished off and went her way home to the Moor.

Mother and Father were both very involved with the church. They were both on the Parochial Church Council, of which Mother was secretary. Mother was also the organist with Father in the choir and both of them ringers. Father's other duties were winding the church clock and stoking the coke-fired boiler for the central heating, though it wasn't called central heating in those days, and I, on occasions climbed the 32 steps to the clock room to help Father wind the clock. It wouldn't quite run for seven days so Father wound it on Sundays and again on Fridays after ringing practice, although we weren't allowed to ring for the first part of the war, from 13 June 1940, partly because the German airships (Zeppelins) flying at night might hear the church bells below them and assume that it was a centre of occupation and drop their bombs. So the ringing of church bells was to be a signal of an invasion and it wasn't until a significant progress had been made in the war at El Alamein, that Winston Churchill said the bells should be rung in celebration from Easter Sunday 25 April 1943.

I started school in 1940/41 and in those days we used to have holidays from school that were tied in to the major festivals like Easter and Whitsun and half days on occasions such as Ash Wednesday when we went across to the church for a short service and then were given the rest of the day off. I was at somewhat of a disadvantage owing to Mother being the headmistress. If I misbehaved the world caved in so that there would be no possibility of my being treated more favourably than the other children. Also I was given errands to run. If Mother had forgotten something or wanted an item to demonstrate a point I would have to run home and get it. One day in July I was on one of these errands when I came across a dead mole, lying in the road. After picking it up and inspecting it, rubbing its fur this way and that to prove that a mole could go backwards without roughing up its coat, I decided that it would be useful for chasing the girls with at playtime, and I was not disappointed; they screamed and ran in all directions. What fun!

Not so much fun was the visit of the dentist, who fixed up his workshop in Fan Higgins' house, Jubilee Cottage, about thirty yards north of the school. All the children had to visit in turn for an inspection of their "gnashers" and any treatment he might consider necessary which started with jamming a spike into each tooth to see if it was hard or soft, then wrenching it back out if he found a soft one. His drill was foot operated by a treadle mechanism and the bit seemed to get extremely hot after he had been treadling away for several minutes. The extractions were quite simple; I don't think he used a hypodermic for the anaesthetic I seem to remember he had a needle with a tiny felt pad impaled on the end of it soaked in something. I can only say I didn't like it, but there was no one prepared to listen if you complained. Then one had to go into another room and sit while he tormented someone else. After a while you would be fetched back into the chair for the tug and twist business then sent back to school. I remember Mother was not amused as we had our own dentist, Frank Harvey at Pen Hill in Yeovil and I think she went and had words with the aforesaid gentleman for pulling a tooth without permission.

The next day was the start of the summer holidays, six weeks of glorious freedom; out in the fields with the tractors and picnic lunches in the cornfields. Some of the workmen had bottles of Taunton cider which they hid beneath the sheaves out of the sun. I quite liked the medium sweet but didn't care for the farmhouse cider that some of them drank. It was like vinegar and made you screw your eyes up and shake your head. When the binder had made a bit of inroad into the standing corn, men would come along and pick up the sheaves, two at a time, one in each hand and stand them up resting against one another with the ears at the top. Then two more against them and then another two. Usually six or eight sheaves would make a little tent called a "stook" that we would wriggle into. Having short trousers in those days, (no jeans around then) the stubble used to play havoc with our knees that stung like blazes when in the bath later on. It was at this time of year that Uncle Frank used to come to see us, for he liked to go pigeon shooting and he would construct a hide to shoot at the birds when they came to land on the stooks to eat the grain in the ears. Father had two shotguns, a double barrelled hammerless twelve bore and an old twelve bore hammer gun with 32" Damascus barrels that was Frank's favourite. Pigeon pie was then on the menu with the inevitable lead shot content which people removed from their mouths with finger and thumb and dropped into the saucer provided.

More School

This idyllic existence was over all too quickly and we were back at school again, to be met by this disgusting smell. No one knew what it was or where it was and nearly a whole morning was lost trying to find it. Eventually, as a last resort the order was given "Everyone empty your desks." The hinged lids were lifted for inspection and the two teachers were going around like bloodhounds, sniffing the air and gradually getting closer and closer. "It's coming from back here somewhere." Then they got to my desk. Right underneath the bottom-most book was something flat, black and furry with a disgusting looking stain spreading from it half way across the bottom of the desk. It was the mole! Or at least what was left of it. Maggots had devoured most of the softer parts. It was removed with a pair of tongs and taken away, then, how to get rid of the smell? Another lesson learned. Mother found a lid of a tin into which she poured some eau de cologne, placed it in the desk, set fire to it and closed the desk top. It didn't actually get rid of the smell, it just altered it and it now smelled weird. I was made to keep that desk until I left the school in 1946 when I won a scholarship to go to Crewkerne Grammar School.

A thing that always puzzled me about girls was why did they like being upside down? In the playground they would spend ages doing handstands against the wall of the Manor Farm cowstalls, which was the boundary wall on the south side. It wasn't a thing that the boys ever did. The girls would tuck their skirts up the legs of their knickers, or not bother, and up they'd go. Of course we were segregated by an iron fence and wouldn't have dared to interfere with teacher looking out of the window. The boys contented themselves by kicking a tennis ball around. Most of the boys wore boots, and I can remember tormenting my Mother until she bought me a pair as well. They made a grand noise when walking on the classroom floor!

The two classrooms were heated by huge Tortoise stoves that burnt coke, a residue of coal that had been heated to extract the coal gas. These stoves were guarded by tall iron frames to keep the children at a safe distance; they were also used to dry the dark blue gabardine mackintoshes that were worn by the children who had walked across the fields from Pendomer or Hardington Marsh some 2½ miles away. Later on in the war the children were collected and delivered by taxi, driven by Irwin Partridge from the Moor.

We had hot meals delivered every day in aluminium containers and a third of a pint of milk each, which I hated and did my best to give it to someone else, as I did my semolina which we seemed to have on too regular occasions.

Hardington School: From the left, Guy Fawkes with beard and lantern is yours truly, and next to me, going along the back row is Jean Lanham; slightly in front of her is Mervyn Berry and the Scots Guardsman is David Winter. Audrey Stidson comes next with Robert White and Jean Axe, hiding behind Richard Voizey's pointed hat. Next to her is Heather Spearing and the cow girl is June Voizey, standing behind Betty Hughes as Britannia who is next to Angela Partridge and Ann Whetham; between and behind them is Christine Whetham. Standing in front of the Head Teacher (my mother) is the nurse, Margaret Charles and then in the top hat is Margaret Love (an evacuee who never went home after the war). Then we have her bride, Nora Marsh with Valerie Chant standing behind Terry Hawkins on the extreme right.

Starting from the left again we have the soldier, Michael Spearing, with John Spearing standing behind Red Riding Hood, Sylvia Marsh. Next is Janice Langdon and Mary Marsh. The young lady with the big basket is Freda Dowding, then Richard Taylor, Alan Stevens and Shirley Axe. Bill Whetham, the jockey, is standing in front of Margaret Charles, who is next to the diminutive cowboy Roderick Marsh and in the white apron is Josephine Gaylard. Behind Josie is Pauline Marsh and the young lady at the front (not of school age) is Josie Legg who lived in the old thatched post office, now Midway. I haven't yet found anyone who can identify the young lad dressed all in white.

Back Row L-R: Mary Whetham; Angela Partridge; Christine Whetham; Gladys Whetham; Freda Poole; June Voizey; Louise Poole; Jean Axe; Lennie Hillard. *Centre Angels:* Gordon Rendell; Ann Whetham;. *Shepherds:* John White; Ted Charles. *Kings:* Margaret Love; Margaret Hounsell; Betty Hughes. *Joseph and Mary:* Evacuees.

Back Row L-R: Valerie Chant; Colin Charles; Margaret Charles; Robert White; Ann Whetham; Evacuee; Audrey Stidson. Front Row: Christine Whetham; Eileen Chidley; Evacuee; Betty Hughes; Betty Chidley.

My mother was always organising something at the school, like little plays, fancy dress events, country dancing and of course the nativity play with shepherds with tea towel headwear and bath towels around their shoulders. The kings naturally, had cut-out cardboard crowns and curtains for cloaks. Near Christmas we made cards using bits of twig and beech mast painted gold or silver; all sorts of interesting designs were achieved.

One day we arrived at school to find some people selling saving stamps and out in the playground at the front of the school was a large bomb on a stand, it must have been 3 or 4 feet long and people were sticking stamps on it. Why, I wondered would people buy stamps and send them to Hitler; they wouldn't be any good after the bomb had gone off anyway. On reflection I suppose they were soaked off and redeemed for the war effort.

We used to have nature walks around the fields and hedgerows and collect bunches of primroses or cowslips which we took back to school to place in jam jars on the windowsills. We never picked bluebells though, for if we did, they would be as limp as string by the time we got back to school and never recover. Also, we never picked orchids, and there were many varieties that grew in the more remote parts of the village, and still do.

When the autumn came it was time to pick blackberries (which stained our mouths and fingers) nuts (which we reached with the aid of a walking stick, then stored them in a biscuit tin ready for Christmas) and rose hips. We used to go and gather rose hips as a class from school, then take the fruits of our labours back to the classroom where we split them open and removed the seeds that, when dry, made excellent itching powder. The hips were then sent off somewhere to be made into rose hip syrup. Another thing we used to collect as a school were conkers. The biggest ones we used to put in our pockets for our own personal use. A meat skewer, and a piece of string with a knot in the end were the other essential ingredients for a game of conkers. We were told at the time that they were sent off to be made into toothpaste. Since then I have discovered that they could be used as an ingredient for some sort of explosive. I wonder which was the case?

Talking of skewers, another plant that was in full bloom at that time was the spindle berry. I was told that the old fashioned wooden meat skewers were made from the timber. It seems strange that a plant with a poisonous berry should be used in the butchery trade for sticking in meat. Poison has reminded me of the time I was walking home from my Aunt Addie's at West Coker, Mother's sister. I had started coming up Chur Lane when I heard something screaming really loudly. I couldn't make out where it was coming from until I saw, in the middle of the lane, a huge adder with a frog in its mouth and it was the frog that was screaming. I gave it a very wide berth and ran up the steep lane as fast as I could until I was out of breath. I think it was the first adder that I had seen, but I recognised it immediately for having seen pictures of them in Mother's encyclopaedias. Slow worms were quite common, especially in the churchyard where the grass didn't get disturbed much. The churchyard was mainly a conservation area in those days because there was long grass, Ox Eye daisies, (Thunder Daisies we used to call them), and many scented wild flowers and weeds. This was accepted as the norm, not like today with motor mowers and not a weed in sight. Then there was Harvest Festival. What a riot of colour and smells! Vegetables lined the aisles, apples of all kinds filled the air with a gorgeous aroma, flowers and sheaves of corn filled every corner and the singing of the traditional harvest hymns bring memories flooding back. You don't get the same effect from a tin of beans or half a dozen eggs that seems to be favourite these days. Most people grew their own food then and seemed more connected to the land. Also, I think, they were more grateful for what they had and went to church to thank God for it.

I had a bout of bronchitis that kept me in bed for a couple of weeks and gave me an opportunity for reading and I loved reading. I remember reading the whole of Arthur Ransome's *Great Northernin* one sitting, not stopping for dinner even. As my mother was a teacher, our house was full of reference books As a result of all this reading I was stuffed with knowledge on all subjects and must have been a right pain on returning to school where I would hold forth on any subject raised; but it has held me in good stead for any quiz occasion that comes up I must confess. But what a "pratt" I must have seemed when teacher asked for the name of a furry animal that flies. The rest of the class said bat. I said flying fox and had an argument with the teacher who had never heard of one. Whereon I explained it was the Australian fruit bat. God, what a bore!

West Coker

One of the traditions in our household was to walk over to West Coker to Auntie Addie's for New Year's Day tea. Her husband, Uncle Albert, was my favourite uncle and Dennis, their son, my favourite cousin who was nine years older than me. Well Auntie always made a sponge cake with pink icing and into the icing were pressed these little coloured ball bearings that were harder than lead shot. The balls were always arranged in the shape of a star. Well, as we sat down to tea and a slice of cake, Father arrived in the car to take us home and he was persuaded to sit down to enjoy a cup of tea and a slice of cake. Auntie then turned to me and said, "Would you like another slice of cake dear ?" I said "No", Mother said "No what?" I said "No fear" and Father hit me under the ear.

Auntie had one or two special treats that I found nowhere else; lemonade made from Eiffel Tower lemonade crystals and little

West Coker 'Brook Villa'.

square sponge cakes made especially for putting in trifles. She also had a sweet jar with some greyish brown mud in the bottom that stood on the window sill in the sun and bubbled every now and again. She said it was Ginger Beer but wouldn't let me try it. Her bread was always kept in an earthenware crock in the cupboard under the stairs and I swear it tasted better than any other bread I ever had, even though we had the same baker, Almy Gould who used to deliver to West Coker and Hardington.

Auntie's house was the one down the track by the side of the Castle Inn. It was called "Brook Villa" or No. 60, High Street, it was built in 1902 by Mother's father, Mr. Tucker. He originated from Portland and came to West Coker to be apprenticed to William Harvey who was a blacksmith, wagon builder, wheelwright and undertaker. He subsequently married Harvey's younger daughter. He also had a son, Roy, who was a painter and decorator, who we didn't see a lot of. He was very artistic, slightly effeminate and very delicate in his movements. He married May and lived in the western house of the block opposite the West Coker Rectory.

The workshop and forge used to fascinate me, and I would spend ages working the old treadle wood lathe making the wheels go round and pumping the handle on the blacksmith's bellows that made a loud snorting noise when the handle went down, making little bits of coal dust jump up into the air from the hearth and a soft chuckling sort of noise when the handle went back up. There was a huge anvil set on a log that was once the base of an elm tree and tools hung all the way around it. The north window that went the whole width of the workshop and forge was again made from the glass plates from the old plate cameras and overlooked the stream from the mill up the road. A really solid looking work bench ran the full width of the workshop with all sorts of fascinating things in boxes under it. There were brass coffin handles and rolls of paper frieze, like you find round Christmas cake, only black and silver, to fix around the top edge of a coffin to cover the tack heads that held the lining in place. Auntie didn't seem too impressed when I took these indoors to show her what I had found and ask what they were for. So I asked uncle Albert and he told me.

Outside the workshop on the ground was a huge circular piece of iron, like a washer but 5'6" (1.7m) in diameter called a bonding plate that was used when they put the heated bonds, or iron tyres, on the wagon wheels. I would love to have been able to have seen the place when they were actually making wagons there. My mother's job when she was a girl was to go around the hot metal tyre with a watering can to stop the wheel from catching fire.

After Dennis' parents died, the lathe disappeared, Dennis having no use for it; but the other items remained until he died in 1983 aged 56. The property was then bought by David Neal who owned the garage in the village with his brothers and sister. I took away the bellows and bonding plate before the sale, hoping

Bonding plate.

to make use of them in some way. The bellows were subsequently stolen, but the bonding plate went on to a most illustrious address. It was bought on Saturday 10 May 2014 by Greg Rowland of Mike Rowland, Wheelwrights and Coachbuilders by appointment to the Queen, of Colyton in Devon It seems that this particular example had exclusive features making it an extremely sought after item, being larger than the norm of 5' (1.5m), tapered towards the centre and with a raised lip. It was taken away by a big pick-up truck bearing the Royal Coat of Arms towing an equally impressive flatbed trailer. I hope Her Majesty will make good use of it.

To get back to Uncle Albert, who was very naughty. I used to wait for him to come home from work on the Safeway's bus. He was a store man in Males' Garage in Manor Road in Yeovil. They were the Vauxhall dealers. He was getting off the bus one Saturday lunchtime when his lunch bag caught the chromium plated CTC fire extinguisher clipped just inside the door and it fell into the road. The conductress, who used to ride on the step and got off first, said "You've dropped your flask." Uncle said "Thanks," and put it in his bag. I still have it! He always had time to play with me and when no one was looking, used to give me a drop of "Squirt", He kept a barrel of cider in the cupboard beneath the stairs. Father used to get extremely annoyed at this. He used to tell me about the bad things that drink did to people and he really disapproved of drinking altogether. Uncle Albert was very wise and gave me lots of advice, such as "When you're using a hammer boy, always catch hold the handle with two hands, then you won't hit your fingers." Another useful one was, "Never you buy a three-wheeler car, lad, 'cos if there's a hole in the road you're bound to hit it with one of your wheels." If ever I asked him where he had been, it was always "Down to Glanvilles Wooton and back round Buckhorn Weston." He used to pronounce it Glandl Zooton an' Buckhorn Wesson. If anyone asked him where something was if they couldn't find it, it was always "Down bottom of the stairs in the bucket." One that Mother disapproved of was "Poop again Daddy, make the baby laugh" and his parting shot was "Thank Mother for the rabbit." I've never forgotten them and relate some of them when the occasion lends itself.

Dennis, being nine years older, was my mentor and whatever he did I tried to copy except for one day when he did something quite extraordinary. He placed a Stephens ink bottle on the lawn and a golf ball on the top of it. Then, taking careful aim with a golf club he whacked it straight through the side of the conservatory. Uncle Albert came out and did something I had never seen before; he kicked Dennis up the backside. We used sometimes to walk up the main road towards Crewkerne to the mill pond. There was an iron gate in the wall leading over a bridge to the bank the other side where we used to fish for minnows or sticklebacks. Dennis made a minnow trap by having an old champagne bottle, one of those with a deep depression in the bottom, he knocked out the central knob, leaving in effect a glass funnel. This was baited with something nice for the fish, corked and lowered to the bottom of the mill pond where inquisitive fish would swim in through the tapered entrance and then couldn't find their way out. One then held the bottle over a large jam jar and pulled out the cork. Job done!

The Flexible Flyer

Now, when the new Rectory was built, the old one, renamed Hardington House, was bought by Brigadier York who had a black Cocker Spaniel answering to the name of Arpee, spelled ARP for Air Raid Precautions and as he had a couple of outbuildings empty Father persuaded him to allow our car and the binder to occupy the spaces. They were open fronted and I often used to go over there

Sled.

and sit on the binder playing "Hangar Pilots," pretending the binder was a bomber flying over Berlin.

One day whilst doing this I noticed a broken toboggan lying in the corner and asked Mrs York if I could have it. After conferring with the Brigadier she said if it was broken it was no good and I could do what I liked with it, so I took it home.

Shortly afterwards, Uncle George came to stay and had a look at it. Father, with his new welding skills, repaired the broken runner and Uncle George completely refurbished it and it looked magnificent. It was an American Flexible Flyer, a two-seater job. When Brigadier York saw me with it, he immediately wanted it back and made Father's life a misery until it was returned, saying that it wasn't the sledge he meant me to have. He had Mr and Mrs Trustrum working for them who had a daughter, Avril, who in the meantime he told to try to persuade me to let her take it home, but I didn't consider that a good idea. I remember Mr Trustrum had a very old Standard car, late 1920s I should think, which he changed for a motorcycle combination which he had the greatest difficulty in driving in a straight line. He drove it into the bank three times going up Rectory Lane, then gave up and pushed it back into the old Rectory. But the Brigadier didn't know that subsequently when Father was asked to do a job for him that included in the price was the cost of restoring the toboggan. Many years later I saw one in the saleroom in Crewkerne and bought it. Now my grandchildren use it and make full use of its steerable properties to avoid frozen mole hills.

The Yorks had the Kelly family living in as house keeper and handyman; there were two children, one a girl called Clare and I think the boy's name was Richard; we used to play in the shrubbery of the big house taking care to keep away from the well, used by the gardener. There was a rustic summer house and a big patch of bamboo that we thought would be ideal for bows and arrows but proved to be most unsuitable. Richard came over one afternoon to play and I had a steam engine that seemed to get very hot and sprayed boiling water everywhere, especially when I operated the whistle so I stood it on a metal tray where, when in motion, it used to hop about all over the place. It was heated by a burner running on methylated spirits. This particular afternoon it started to slow down and I looked underneath the boiler where the burner appeared to have gone out, so I refuelled it from the can of methylated spirit. There was a loud "Poof" and the can flew out of my hand. Father, who had been sitting at the dining table in the next room jumped up, ran out into the kitchen and gave me a big hug, which I thought was rather unusual, he was not usually that affectionate, but it seems I was unaware that I was on fire. He flung me into the dining room, grabbed a heavy mackintosh off the coat rack and put out the burning can, while Richard looked on from the safety of the pantry doorway where he had taken refuge. Shortly afterwards, I believe the Kellys returned to Ireland.

Another service Father provided was the supply of petrol (Pool) in those days when all the various suppliers such as Shell, BP, & Esso, all delivered to a central depot from where it was distributed to the pumps. We had a Shell Mk 5 pump which was a hand operated one with two half gallon glass measuring bottles which filled alternately and when one was full it turned over to the other, which filled while the other was emptying. We also had tanks for paraffin and tractor vaporising oil and drums of lubricating oil and methylated spirit. The paraffin and meths were for the Primus stoves that many households had for cooking.

Then there was the battery charging equipment for re-charging the glass accumulators for the radios and starter batteries for vehicles and motor cycles. This necessitated the storage of acid and distilled water in glass "carboys" (large round bottles resting in wire baskets lined with straw). The ones containing acid had ground glass stoppers while the distilled water was only sealed by a cork. I used to tell if a jug contained acid or water by spilling a tiny drop on the floor; if it fizzed, it was acid, if it didn't, it was water. As well as stocking the 120 volt high tension batteries and the grid bias batteries for radios there were cycle parts, torches, tyres and all sorts of interesting things, and I learned how to read Vernier gauges and micrometers. The garage had an inspection pit that I used to use as a hiding place when playing hide and seek with friends. I would slide one of the boards back, slip down through and slide the board back into place. The finders would often come and stand right above me, but I was never found. There was a loft above that was reached by a vertical ladder in the north west corner. I spent hours up there; it had a galvanised roof and I hung a garden hammock between two of the collar beams and when it was a warm day in the summer with a storm of rain hammering on the roof I would lie in the hammock listening to the rain and would be fast asleep in minutes, until Mother stuck her head up through the trap door to call me in for tea.

We had a transformer running our radio off the mains which produced an annoying background hum, but it didn't detract from the enjoyment too much. I used to listen to Children's Hour hosted by Uncle Mac, Derek McCulloch and *ITMA* (It's That Man Again), with Tommy Handley. I enjoyed Cyril Fletcher and his odd odes, and *Much Binding* with Dickie Murdoch and Kenneth Horne was another favourite with their songs about Much Binding in the Marsh. They did one about the Yeovil Town Football Club in 1949 who were being classed as Giant Killers by the media as they had beaten Bury and Sunderland at home on their way to the cup final, then had drawn Manchester United away, it went something like this.

Down in the jungle, chanting every day,
You can hear the natives all say;
"Yeovil's playing Manchester,
They haven't got a hope.
Are you listening Yeovil? No slope!"

Yeovil's football pitch had a notorious slope which resulted in the ground being eight feet higher on the N/E corner and was looked at by a visiting team as a handicap to those that didn't play there regularly.

It's now a Tesco Supermarket so that excuse no longer applies.

Our water in those days came from Odcombe and was fed to a reservoir at Pen Lane and then piped to the village. On Friday mornings a group of women used to meet at "Aunt Blanche Axe's" in the middle house of the three Portman cottages at Broadstone. Each of these members was delegated to read a specific portion of the *Western Gazette* and then discuss it over a cup of tea. It was remarked by some that Aunt Blanche's tea tasted better than their own even though they all got their tea from Aunt Nance Voizey's shop up Broadstone Lane. Nance was usually known as Annie, and the shop had been there for years, Annie's mother ran it all through the First World War. A lovely long, low, thatched cottage with huge flagstones outside. She was a very careful woman; when her nephew, Herbie Voizey the butcher, called in with his two children she would generously ask them if they would like a sweet.

"Would 'ee like a pop m'dears," then if the reply was in the affirmative she would take a small square of paper and roll it around her fingers to make a cone then turn up the end. Sweets were added, being frequently weighed on the counter scales until they just balanced at a quarter pound, then after Herbie had handed over the money she would take two sweets out of the bag and hand to the children. She had her "come uppence" though, because the kids used to go round to the back door while she was busy serving someone and pick up a couple of lemonade bottles and bring them to the front door to collect the sixpence deposit that was due on each of them. She had all sorts of things in that shop, some I wondered what they were for; Carter's Little Liver Pills for instance and little Imps throat sweets that were so hot we spat them out. Aunt Nance also played the harmonium in the chapel up in the High Street. I could never understand why they needed two churches in the village; why didn't everyone go to the same one? Bill Delamont who lived at the top of Bridgeclose Hill, and was a ringer at the church, used to leave at ten to six and walk briskly up through the High Street to the chapel service at six o' clock. Still, he was a useful Tenor ringer.

Wells, Pubs and a Feather Bed

Anyway, to get back to Aunt Blanche's and the Friday group. It was then revealed that Aunt Blanche Axe's tea was made with water from the well outside the front door. Many households had their own well and those that didn't could use the parish pump just below the chapel in the High Street. Most of the wells were relatively shallow, but the one at Rydons was quite deep, necessitating in a platform being made half way down to mount the pump on. A suction pump can only lift water 32', which is the maximum that atmospheric pressure can push it up. If you take Barry House as an example, the original well was in the front garden, if you look carefully at the front wall on the corner, there is a load-bearing arch built into it to spread the weight of the wall past the extremities of the well. This was superseded by a new well dug at the side of the ditch adjoining Wimborough Lane; you can see the pipe from it running across the ditch, then this pipe is encased in a bigger pipe going across the stream in Rag Orchard. This is to protect the inner one from frost. Then halfway up the lane there was a pump to draw the water from the well and then force it up to the farm house.

Up at Underhill, or Black House as it was more commonly known, the cottage above North Lane on the way to West Coker had a nice brick-lined well, but the water didn't taste very nice so Ed Charles would every morning on his way to work put a bucket under a little dribble of water coming out of the bank about 100 yards down the Eastern side of North Lane, then when he came back from work he would pick up the now full bucket of nice spring water and carry it home. Sometimes some children, to amuse themselves, would tip up the bucket and if the people living in the adjacent cottage failed to notice it, Ed would have no water to take back, so would replace the bucket and return later in the hope that it had refilled. Fortunately they made a lot of cider up there, so he did have something to drink when he arrived home.

Talking of drink, there used to be five pubs in Hardington. Two were at the Moor, the Royal Oak and an older pub, the White

The Royal Oak.

The Old White Horse.

Horse, the building on the left as you stand at the bottom of Pig Hill. Up in the village was the New Inn, and along Barry Lane just before you get to Field View was the Muddy Green, and down at

The Old New Inn.

the Marsh was the Griffin. The last two were just cider houses. I can remember the building of the skittle alley at the New Inn, I like to think that I helped but I was only about five at the time. I still have the putty stuck on the handle of my wheelbarrow that Granddad Tucker made for me. It was Grandfather who made the blackout screens and also a play house at the top of the garden and a sandpit.

There used to be a man called Tommy Backholler who only had one eye who used to live in a shepherd's hut in the orchard at the New Inn. I think he might have been related to Mrs Curtis; he used to help out feeding the pigs and poultry and he had two tricycles one to ride while the other one was in for repair. He used to bring them to Father to sort out. I remember him climbing aboard to go home one Sunday morning and releasing the brake, (we had a steep drive up to the garage with double gates at the bottom.) He gathered speed and then smacked his front wheel against the gate stop in the middle of the drive; possibly having only one eye contributed to his trip over the handlebars and landing in the road.

The bent front forks would now only allow left hand turns and he wanted to go right to go home so he left the trike and walked, not very steadily, across the field, back to his shepherd's hut.

I was standing outside what used to be the White Horse one day with Robbie White and a couple more lads whose names I forget, when Les Tanner came by with his horse and cart. He was a bit of a rag and bone man and used to collect scrap iron etc. On the top of his load he had a mattress and as he went by, Robbie ran out behind the cart and slit the mattress with his pen knife. It was a feather bed and the down started falling out to be picked up by the breeze. Jim Hughes, who was standing in the doorway called back in to his wife,

"Come and have a look at this, Mother. There's feathers coming down from the sky!" The reply came back,

"You've been up Harold Curtis's again han 'ee?" Harold was the landlord of the New Inn where Jim used to spend some time. This discourse brought the situation to the attention of Les who dithered between trying to stop the feathers coming out or chasing us, who by this time had legged it.

Talking of horses, Billy Watts was the blacksmith and his forge was on the right hand side going up the High Street just past the turning to Bishop's Lane. I went in once to see him shoeing a horse and thought the atmosphere wonderful but I didn't like it when he set fire to the horse by holding a red hot shoe against its foot. There was a hiss and clouds of smoke and the smell was dreadful.

Billy had a son Bert, who formed a dance band and went around the villages playing for barn dances. One was held occasionally in the Manor Farm; you went up the outside steps to a long room over the waggon house. At the far end was a stage with a piano and fastened to the wall were two boards in the shape of a church window that displayed the Ten Commandments, which had originally hung on the east wall of the chancel until 1869 when my grandfather and his uncle rebuilt the church and put in an east window instead. Bert played the piano, Don Margetts was on accordion and there was a saxophonist and a drummer, whose names I can't recall.

I used to spend quite a bit of time at Manor Farm and in the holidays I would sometimes, if I couldn't sleep, go up to the farm to watch them milking the cows by hand; the ones that were known to kick the bucket over occasionally would have their legs tied together with a piece of rope that had an eye in one end. The rope was passed around the further leg and crossed over between the legs like a figure of eight, the end passed through the eye, pulled up tight then finished off with a half hitch with the end pulled back through to make releasing more simple. The milk was carried to the dairy in two huge buckets hanging by chains from a wooden yoke, made from ash, resting on the shoulders. The milk was then poured into a high hopper from where it ran down over a corrugated water cooled device before running into a large funnel with a filter cloth in it which was sitting in the top of a milk churn. These churns were collected every morning by a lorry and taken to the milk factory down by Westland's airfield. I remember that one of the milk lorry drivers behaved rather peculiarly, jumping and kicking his leg out and jerking his head. Apparently he suffered from "St Vitus Dance" which I didn't understand. I wondered later how he managed to drive, he also rode a motorcycle. Fortunately, there wasn't too much traffic about or some of his hand signals could have been rather confusing. Milking over, they would invite me in for breakfast and I would still be home before Mother got up. They were always very good to me, and if we were going to London to see Uncle Frank, Father would send me up for a chicken to take with us.

"Mr. Turner, Dad says could we have a chicken to take to Uncle Frank?"

"Course you can me dear. Come along, let's go and get one." And we would go out into the orchard where he would grab one as it went by and wring its neck.

"There you are, how's that?" and he would give me its legs to hold while its wings were still flapping.

U.S. of A.

Then we had the Americans, not to an overpowering extent; a lot of them were hauled up in the park at Montacute House and occasionally came through the village on manoeuvres. I remember being given a lift home from school in a jeep and on one occasion seeing a yellow cable hanging up in the roadside hedge. I followed it for ages but never got to the end of it. I wondered how long it was altogether and what it was for. Probably a field telephone I expect. It was eventually collected by an army lorry with a soldier in the back winding the cable onto a big drum. Every now and then it would snag on a branch in the hedge and they would stop to untangle it before moving on again.

Sometimes they did tracking like we did, only they used a jeep to go on in front and stick little flags in the bank to show where they had gone, then several lorries and jeeps would come chasing after them, until they got to the bottom of Wimborough Lane where a child, who shall remain nameless, had removed the flag to watch the confusion. Some turned left and went up Wimborough Lane, others carried straight on up Partway Lane to Hill Cross where they found another flag to direct them to Haselbury. I remember that there was a lot of shouting when they all came to a standstill. The flag was eventually quickly replaced on Father's instructions after I had shown it to him to see what I had found.

Then there were the convoys of army lorries. We didn't get them at Hardington, but on the main roads they were frequent. If you stood in front of the church tower and looked towards East Chinnock you could see them going up, or down the A30. The first vehicle carried a dark blue flag about eighteen inches long by twelve inches high, usually tied to the nearside door mirror and the last one a green flag the same size tied to the nearside of the rear frame supporting the canvas canopy. They always travelled at a steady thirty miles per hour with a regular distance between them. Affixed to the rear axle, or somewhere around that area, was a white painted disc, about seven inches in diameter.

Because of the blackout, when they were travelling at night with masks over the headlights, this disc was about the only thing the driver could see of the lorry he was following. A convoy of thirty or more vehicles was not uncommon and they drove by droning monotonously, with only the occasional dispatch rider spluttering backwards and forwards to break the rhythm.

The British convoys consisted mostly of Bedford lorries while the Americans had an assortment of Chevrolets, Dodges and Studebakers. The Chevrolets had a peculiar forward sloping windscreen, to lessen the chances of sunlight reflecting off the glass and so giving its position away to the enemy. Many years later, this design was repeated in the rear window of the Ford Anglia 105 E, but I'm sure not for the same reason. My favourites were the Dodge with its smooth streamlined lines and the Studebaker with its long, sloping bonnet.

Occasionally we saw the R.A.F. "Queen Marys"; they were very long trailers built like a Bailey bridge, all open framework hauled by a Bedford Tractor unit. They were designed for hauling complete aircraft fuselages or a pair of wings.

Milk and Eggs

At about that time, one of the lads I went to school with was Colin Charles; he lived at Field View, in Barry Lane. His father, Jack, kept a couple of goats which he used to tether on the roadside grass verges each with iron stakes and chains while he was at work and he used to milk them in the evening when he got home. I asked Colin what goats' milk tasted like.

"Father has it in his tea," he said, "but I don't care for it much; by the time you've strained all the hairs out of it your tea's cold." He also had the dubious fame of being the only person I had ever heard swear at my mother. It was when we were learning to read and we were being asked to make the sounds produced by various letters of the alphabet. Colin was asked, "What does letter "R" say?

"Ar" he said.

"No" replied my mother, "Try again."

"AR." He repeated, more loudly and with feeling.

" No, Colin, you haven't been paying attention." Hoping that he would say " r r".

" Yes it is" he shouted, almost in tears, "It's AR, you bugger." He got his hand slapped for that.

On another occasion we had cards to read; you can tell how advanced we were for we were now reading words of three letters. On one side of the card there were about four words, say PAN, CAT, DOG, TIN, and on the reverse there were pictures of the items so that you could check whether you were correct. No cheating was allowed.

"Now, Colin, what does PAN spell?"

"Frying Pan!" was the reply. Oh dear.

I had never seen anyone climb trees like Colin could, he didn't have a fearful bone in his body. He would shin up the 50 foot trees at the bottom of Wimborough Lane to take an egg out of a rook's nest. He'd then put it in his cap, which he replaced on his head and shin back down the tree. Most of us had egg collections in those days, we'd prick a hole in the egg with a blackthorn and have a piece of fine grass stem to use as a blow pipe to force the insides out. Not always successful; sometimes we squeezed too hard and broke the egg.

Another occupation, slightly earlier in the year was to go around the ponds collecting frogspawn in a jam jar with a string handle held in place with a special knot that only small boys seemed to use; the one at the bottom of Five Acres was usually more fruitful than Millcombe Pond at the bottom of North Lane; once we had captured sufficient (it's very slippery stuff to pick up), then we would take the jars to school and put them in the window sills to watch the little tadpoles form and grow into little frogs. I don't know why but I can't remember any of them getting much past the stage of growing their back legs, perhaps jam jars didn't contain enough oxygen, or enough food. There weren't supermarkets about then with rows of shelves of cat food. Our animals used to eat the same as we did, and on one occasion, vice versa. Mother had got hold of a tin of Red Heart dog food. She turned it out onto a dish and the dog didn't seem very keen so she put it back in the larder, (we didn't have a 'fridge in those days,) then Ransome came in and made a stew for lunch and put the dog meat in as the main ingredient. When Mother came back later and couldn't find the dish with the dog food on enquired what we had been given for dinner.

"Stew," said Father. "It was very good." Mother said nothing.

Talking of ponds, the best ones were at Hardington Marsh on Richard Voizey's farm, there were several all with their own attractions. Moorhens used to nest on them and one occasionally saw a fox curled up asleep under a bush in the sun. Then we would hear a train coming and we'd all run like mad, or at least as fast as our wellington boots caked in mud would allow, to go into one of the tunnels in the railway embankment that were for getting cows from one side of the line to the other. If we had time, we tried to stand as near the centre of the tunnel as possible and then wait for the huge roaring noise as the train went overhead. Another thing we used to do was to put halfpennies on the railway line and wait for a train to go over them, hoping that they would be squashed out to the size of a penny. Sometimes they were vibrated off the line by the approaching locomotive and other times when hit, they would fly up into the air and be lost amongst the ballast. Seldom were we successful in retrieving a squashed one. Sewing needles, held in place with chewing gum (supplied by Uncle Sam), would be pressed into the rail, which was of a softer metal than the needles.

Then, as for noise, there was the air raid siren! The one we used to hear was located alongside the Quicksilver Mail public house at the top of Hendford Hill in Yeovil. It was perched on top of a tall wooden structure which brought it level with the roof. We could hear it quite plainly at Hardington so Lord knows what it sounded like in the houses opposite on West Coker Road. Especially as it seemed to go off more often at night; there was certainly no chance of sleeping through it!

Then one day I was outside Nancy Voizey's shop when one of my friends pulled up on his bicycle.

"The war's over" he said, "They've give it out on the wireless." That must have been 8 May 1945, or was it? Because we were on double summer time we were an hour ahead of CET which meant the war effectively ended at 0100 hrs on the 9th. I went out that evening expecting to see a blaze of light; everyone having taken down their blackout. But no, it was just the same, even if they hadn't put up the blackout they still drew the curtains. Nothing seemed to be any different. I think the first evidence of a change was the removal of the headlamp masks from the cars.

Then, when driving at night you could tell if there was a car coming towards you long before it came into view as you could see the glow in the sky and the reflection of the lights on the telegraph wires. Now the headlamp design keeps the light down on the road and we don't have the phone wires carried individually on poles. Father told me that the cross bars on the poles carrying the insulators were always on the side of the pole facing London. There's a piece of useless information, unless of course you were driving to London and were lost.

A phone call from Uncle Frank suggested that we should all go up to London to see the Victory Parade on 8 June 1946. That seemed too good an opportunity to miss so off we went. I don't remember which part of London we went to but I do remember it was nearly my undoing. We were standing on a corner, and like all the kids I was pushed to the front to get a better view. The procession was going past with the crowd making such a noise, cheering and shouting at the service men and women, when I was suddenly grabbed by the coat collar and dragged violently backwards as a tank, making the turn, got it a little previous and came across the pavement where I had been standing. I didn't know who to thank for saving my life, for by the time I had regained a vertical posture my rescuer was screaming and shouting with everyone else

The war was a great step forward in my upbringing, teaching me the practicalities of make do and mend and how to make something useful out of something that was considered of no further use, patience, and most of all, it taught me to think before I did something and consider all the consequences of my actions.